I0407793

THE IMPOSSIBILITY OF LONELINESS

OF

LONELINESS

• THE SEARCH FOR HOME •

© 2017 Chinle Miller, Maya Kurtz

All rights reserved, including the right of reproduction in whole or in part in any form.

Yellow Cat and the accompanying logo are registered trademarks owned by Yellow Cat Publishing.

www.yellowcatbooks.com

Names, characters, places, and incidents either are the product of the author's imagination or are used fictitiously. Any resemblance to actual persons, living or dead, events, or locales is entirely coincidental.

All photos by Chinle Miller
Front cover design by Alice Sjoberg Design
Back cover design by Chinle Miller

• ALSO BY CHINLE MILLER •

Uranium Daughter

Desert Rats: Adventures in the American Outback

*In Mesozoic Lands: A Guide to the Mesozoic Geology of
Arches and Canyonlands National Parks*

The Bud Shumway Mystery Series:

The Ghost Rock Cafe

The Slickrock Cafe

The Paradox Cafe

The No Delay Cafe

The Silver Spur Cafe

The Ice House Cafe

The Rattlesnake Cafe

The Beartooth Cafe

The Melon Rind Cafe

• FOR •

Toni and John

And for Moki, Weezee, and Cassie

CONTENTS

1   *Preface*

Part I: Going Home
4   Homecoming
7   Jessie's Twist
9   Hondu Country
13   Alien Camp
17   Green River Desert
20   Drowned Hole Draw
22   A Steady Cold Wind Bearing Ravens
26   Bullish Dreams
29   Going, Always Going

Part II: At Altitude
32   Two Rivers
35   The Impossibility of Loneliness
38   May the Wolf Be with You
43   River One: Red Water
46   River Two: Green Water
48   River Three: Bear Water
50   Queen Anne's Lace

Part III: I Dream of Bears
56   That Thin Space of Existence
62   A Conspiracy of Ravens
63   Mt. Sneffels

68   That Melancholic Divide
74   A Paradoxical Pair
78   Whatever Makes You feel Alive
84   We Can Talk About It When We All Get
       To Heaven
88   Orion's Gone A'Hunting
92   Moki's Gone
97   Into the Triangle
105   Heirloom Honeysuckle
108   Star Bears

Part IV: Northern Dreams
114   A Bear Story
116   Bear Dreams
123   Arctodus Simus
131   An Absolute, Catastrophic Collision of
       Events
134   The Wolves of Nahanni
143   The Lost Land of Beringia
147   Aurora
153   She Who Walks Leaving No Tracks
162   Riding the Wind
170   Ursus Arctos Horribilis
177   Finding Yet Another Piece of My Home
185   Over the Edge
191   Into the Depths
197   Valley of Dreams
202   Horribilis

208   *Epilogue*

PREFACE

When you stand in the immensity of the natural world and realize how utterly insignificant you are, only then are you truly free.

There are many stories on this planet, and so begins this, a story carved into the white bark of aspen trees like the lonely Basque sheepherders carved their names and messages: "Joaquin stuck 3 days mud."

It's a story that turns like the wooden wheels that creak through rough sagebrush flats, carrying the old wagons stacked with rough ponderosa pine from the mountain, yellowbellies for building the long low ranch houses solid to withstand snow blown across the mountain by wild winds.

It's a story of tenacity and love and wild blue iris, and a story of the search for home, that place bound with the sap from the cut trees, bound with that same fragrance that surrounds you after a long cool mountain rain filled with blue lupine.

It's a story of mountain verticality, of thin air that catches you unawares and tries to wring out your lungs, of the blinding-white light of glaciers against summer bluebird skies.

And it's a story of desert—desert beauty and desert empty. A story of rock and time and dust.

And a story of bears.

It's a story we all could tell, one we all know, one we all feel, the same story that fells some of us like those tall ponderosas were felled.

It's a story of the lost, of those wandering on a small planet spinning around a massive sun that bombards us with rays that fill the northern skies with soft undulating auroral colors with no descriptions.

It's a story of time that flows slow. A story of our search for that place where we belong, where we step out of our worn boots, weary, wonderfully happy to have arrived.

It's a story of the search for home.

A story with no ending.

And so it begins.

PART I

GOING HOME

Green River Desert, Utah

HOMECOMING

Early October, headed west, I can feel the tautness in my shoulders relax the minute the Big Empty embraces me, as soon as the city of Grand Junction, Colorado is no longer in my rear-view mirror.

I pass a sign that reads, "Rabbit Valley," and I recall camping here many times, some not-so-great times, living in my pickup, no home to come from or return to.

Times are better, at least for now, and I'm on my way home, back home to my beloved desolation, the desert, to that hardscrabble little town of Green River, Utah, a town of many hidden charms, some so hidden no one knows they exist.

I think of the quiet there, of the unpretentious people, of the lonesome train whistles at night followed by the clickety-clack of heavy metal wheels rolling down the tracks, pushing the quiet ahead of them and dragging the noise behind as they pass old abandoned brick buildings with the words "Billiards" in faded white paint.

The Big Empty stretches on and on, 100 miles, no services, nothing but a great sense of hope and freedom, those two dreams that brought my ancestors to America from Ireland and Scotland and other distant lands reeking of too much habitation for too long.

And now, I'm a sailor on a sea of alkali hills and adobe flats, all paralleled by the longest east-west range in the world, the Book Cliffs, called simply "the Books" by the locals. John Wesley Powell named them the Azure Cliffs when he came floating through on the Green River, naming things, but the old name used by the early trappers stuck.

The Books. Tall cliff faces that stretch for over 200 miles through Utah into Colorado, laced with deep wild canyons and even deeper and wilder mountain lions and bears. Lots of bears.

I'm going home.

Hot summer has left the desert parched and worn, but the early hints of autumn now bathe everything in a faded light, golden rabbitbrush catching in wind and dancing.

Finally, I see it, a long low outline to the west, the San Rafael Swell, banded by the sharks' teeth of the San Rafael Reef. Here there be dragons, wild horses, and burros.

I smile. Every time I come back and see that wild skyline, every cell in my body feels joy, and I want to kiss the earth.

I'll spend the winter here in my stronghold from civilization. The very thought of endless days wandering the wildlands, of exploring waterless washes and rocky cliffs and dinosaur tombs makes me catch my breath in gratitude for my good fortune.

Coming home, homecoming.

I now see the long-abandoned buildings on the high hills near town, a desultory off-white against the deep dusty blues of the Books, part of the Cold War missile range that boomed the town in the 60s and 70s. I take the Green River exit and roll on down that lost highway to my little lost town.

The old Hank Williams song "Lost Highway" always returns to me when I come back. I sing it all winter while here, relishing being lost—lost in the Big Empty.

Crossing the bridge over the Green River, I cruise on down the long drag into town, turn by the big tall Athena missile in the park, go one more block, then I'm home, the little rental bungalow across the street from the Mormon Church with its tall spike pointing to the sky, calling to Saints and part-time Saints alike.

"How many people do you know with a big white Athena missile out their door, poised to take flight?" I ask my cousin Davie on the phone.

He pauses, answers, "Trick question."

The dogs tumble from the pickup and rush around madly, sniffing and peeing on bushes, wagging tails. They know this place, know what it means—freedom. Days of running and chasing and digging.

I open the door to the old dingy house and am greeted by the sound of a mouse skittering under the cupboards. Windows are dusty, and house still smells faintly of the hot-buttered-rum candle still sitting half-burned on the mantle.

Nothing's changed. Except now we're home.

JESSIE'S TWIST

Only a few days back, and I'm already longing for motion. I load up the dogs and go for a drive.

It's hard to describe the loneliness out here in this wild country. Driving along some backroad, it jumps in beside you from nowhere, unexpected, and won't get out, its presence permeating everything.

I turn on the radio and hum along, trying to ignore my desultory passenger, but somehow that seems to empower it, to make me think of it even more. I finally give up and acknowledge its presence.

"What makes you want to hang out here with me?" I touch my hat brim congenially in its direction. "You kind of lose your edge when you're not alone, you know."

I imagine the reply: *Oh, I know, sometimes I just want to show you the country, its depth, how it can really feel.*

I counter, "Well, thanks, I guess."

And so we drive on, together in silence, me and this deep loneliness, until eventually something happens—a small herd of white-rumped pronghorn antelope appears on a hill. The clouds open, and light dances across the tips of the immense flatirons of the Reef behind them.

I stop the truck and get out, sand pushing into that pesky hole in my boot. A redtail hawk flames across blue sky. Suddenly, I feel like I'm part of a rainbow, light filtering around me, through me, a spectrum of bright color.

Wind blows through the motion of nearby rabbitbrush, and I think about how some say you can search forever for the meaning of life and never find it. Others say you have to make your own meaning, make sense of it all some way or another.

But for me, for now anyway, it all suddenly makes sense, this texture of gigantic sandstone sharks' teeth, these frighteningly deep potholes and impossible slot canyons, the vertical streaks of black rain clouds brushing against towers of white stone.

Back in the truck, I realize I've somehow ditched my passenger. Alone again, I smile, knowing loneliness will be back around when least expected or wanted.

Evening sunset fire blazes across the shoulders of distant Ghost Rock. A flock of powder-blue pinion jays wheels across the sky, flying through a distant span of rainbow.

I look in the rearview mirror to see a mirage of lake reflecting a clear band of light from setting sun. I'm at Jessie's Twist, where the old highway from Hanksville to Green River twists up through the candy-cane Morrison cliffs.

The first star of night appears, alone, soon to be joined by a multitude.

HONDU COUNTRY

It's now mid-November and feels like something's soon changing, that feeling of impending storm, of winter edging into the blue horizon with black clouds. I know if I want to go to Hondu Arch, it's now or never.

Hondu Country is a vast expanse on the south section of the San Rafael Swell, southwest of Green River, and was named for Hondu Arch, which in turn was named after the small oblong part of a lariat that holds the loop.

Apparently the arch looks like a hondu, and I've been wanting to go see it for myself, but for some reason it feels like a far distant place, kind of akin to Mongolia. Yet it's only maybe all of 40 miles distant—but that 40 miles is rugged and has a most lonely feel to it.

I've had other days when I thought I'd go, but somehow never did. Why does it feel so remote? I've driven near there and flown over it, and it wasn't really all that far. Maybe it's the fact that winter's nearly here.

I decide to go tomorrow and put some survival gear in the pickup—an extra sleeping bag, a stove, some food and water, that kind of thing.

The next day, I'm up bright and early. The weather looks superb, but I procrastinate—a second cup of coffee, then tuning in the weather radio. Finally, I decide it's now or never, as a big storm is coming in tomorrow, according to the weatherman.

I load up the dogs and head out, wondering why I picked the day before a big storm to go. Must have a subconscious desire for adventure—or something like that.

The Swell can seem like the end of the earth, yet it's not, as there are usually a few ranchers, dirt bikers, and hikers there, especially in the fall and spring. But this late in the season, there's probably nobody up there.

I climb the shoulders of the Swell, up, up through Spotted Wolf Canyon, where the highway was blasted out to allow passage through the once too-tight canyon.

The highway winds and climbs, and soon on top, I can see Mexican Mountain and Buckhorn Wash country and the Wedge off to my right. Any hints of Hondu Country are hidden by the Swell itself, still higher on my left.

I soon turn off the highway and head west on a wide dirt road with cattle wandering along its flanks. The wind is picking up, creating little squalls of dust, precursor to the coming storm. I suspect this one will shut down most of the roads up here where the elevation is near 7000 feet, a good 3000 feet higher than the Green River Desert below.

The road heads south, and I see the Aquarius Plateau in the far distance, as well as the Moroni Slopes. To the west a rock formation known as the Family sticks its collective heads above the horizon until they're finally in full sight. A little two-track road takes off to the rocks, but I resist the urge and keep going.

Now near the highest point on the Swell, I can see into Mussentuchit country, beautiful badlands at the lower reaches of the Swell to the west that must not be touched.

I've forgotten my map, but the road is well-marked, and I'm soon gradually descending until the road narrows and drops off in earnest into badlands, twisting and turning, and all seems more and more remote, this empty place on the map, a stretch of wild country that goes miles and miles, no civilization anywhere. Desert, you are my not-so-secret love.

Now I've dropped down into an old uranium mining area, tailings spilling out of old doghole mines, crying for their lost past. I see a wild mare and her colt watching me from a rise, and I stop to get photos, but they're off running, though not very fast, curious. I get a few photos before they're gone into the twisty badlands. A hard life, but free.

I'm in the bottom of a vast canyon system, in the drainage of Muddy Creek, a small stream that hails from the slopes of the distant Wasatch Plateau (not to be confused with the Wasatch Mountains, an entirely different geologic province). How such a small waterway could carve such an extensive canyon system speaks of lots of time, deep geologic time, to do such work.

Road ends, and I stop in a grove of stately ancient Fremont cottonwoods, still bearing part of the crackled remnants of their autumn leaves.

The dogs get out and sniff around. We walk down to Muddy Creek, and they wade in the cold slow waters, only a few inches deep.

I look up to the cliffs above me to suddenly see the arch, barely holding the cliffs together.

All is quiet, and peace flows through the canyons along with the waters of Muddy Creek, on down to the greater waters of the Dirty Devil River at Hanksville and then eventually to the more stately Colorado River.

I'm quiet, carefully holding this very precious moment in time, knowing it will soon pass with the coming winter storm.

And I have no idea of the magnitude of another storm on its way, a storm coming from Alaska that will blow my life into a completely different direction.

ALIEN CAMP

Utah's San Rafael Swell is an island in a sea of wildlands, a place of strange night lights and satellites wobbling across the sky in predetermined paths.

And so, one late November night, my cousin Davie comes to visit, and we camp on that island, near the Wick-iup, known as Molly's Nipple in the days before political correctness, and we begin an experiment in scaring ourselves.

I've always been close to both Davie and his sister, Janie, even though the two have their differences. Janie and Davie and I go way back—we've climbed Colorado peaks together, slogged through epic rainstorms, windstorms, and sandstorms together, even managed to survive innumerable family holidays together.

But Janie now lives far away in Hawaii, and it's just me and Davie this time. Our minds are too much alike, perhaps, and our evening conversations are pretty predictable.

We start out talking about the day, what we did and how we did it and all that. Then, as dusk falls, we talk about other past days. By the time the bowl of night opens, we've moved to Earth's mysteries, like the Great Pyramids and the Desert Hum and the Yellowstone Whispers. By the time the Milky Way blazes across the night sky and the fire's burned low, we're inevitably discussing the vast inexplicable universe.

This night was no different, except we decide we want to photograph a UFO. Since one doesn't come around to oblige us, we create our own.

How does one create a UFO? Davie digs out his headlamp and begins experimenting, while I prop my camera on a stump. I set it with a very long shutter time, and he begins whirling the light, dancing around, doing his best to create something weird.

We review the photos, decide they're not enough. We add colored lights by putting a candy wrapper around the light, and he twirls with that, setting his light to strobe. He then goes inside his tent and does dance-like movements with the light, which shines through the colored blue nylon. He sets the light by an old pinion tree, and we film the glowing tree. He stands next to the truck mirror and makes reflections of himself and the light. He puts the light in his mouth, sticks it inside his cupped hands, jumps over it, does everything strange he can think of.

We have a habit of naming our camps, names like Savannah Camp, Cowpie Camp, and Washtub Camp. We name this one Alien Camp. The photos are weird and bizarre, just what we want. Digital cameras are wonderful that way, you get instant results.

Pleased with ourselves, we then sit around and talk about real UFOs, or supposed real ones, as opposed to our newly minted photos of them.

Later, back in Colorado, Davie calls and breaks the bad news.

He's just out of jail with a DUI. He was in for three days, dreaming of aliens the whole time, he tells me. Now he truly understands and appreciates freedom and wonders if I could somehow arrange for an alien abduction before he goes to court.

"They'll probably send me to jail for awhile, but I'll get out soon," he tries to reassure me.

"No hurry," I joke.

He replies, "I'll be fine. I actually got home from the party OK, then remembered I'd forgotten my housemate, so went back. That's when they busted me. It's all his fault."

Silence.

"OK, it's a good lesson for me, no more treating angst with demon whiskey."

Silence, but I smile.

"Janie's disowned me—for the millionth time."

Later, he calls again, and he's been sentenced.

"How soon will you be out?" I ask. "What about the dogs?"

"They'll stay at a friend's. They'll be OK," he answers. "Watch for the Indian paintbrush to bloom, that's when I'll be out."

I can't talk. I'm all choked up.

He continues, "Send me some good books."

"What kind?"

"Books on great escapes—Houdini, Butch Cassidy, that sort of thing."

I laugh, and we say goodbye.

I send him books for the duration, "Moby Dick,""Gone with the Wind,""War and Peace,"lengthy books.

And one slim volume of desert wildflowers, complete with photos of Indian paintbrush in bloom.

GREEN RIVER DESERT

The weather radio announces another in a series of icy winter storms in a voice as hollow as the frozen hoofprint of a curly-chested Angus bull.

That particular bull is a bit of a pain, as he haunts one of the few stretches I can easily access when everything's frozen up in this big empty desert. And frozen-up often means all of December and January and into February, more than two months of keeping an eye for that big bull, though he's probably harmless.

What he finds out there to subsist on is beyond me, but he grazes along the road all winter until the rancher he belongs to brings him in for whatever bulls do in the spring.

Today's the winter solstice and I'm happy for it, and a feeling of optimism, along with cabin fever, draws me outside, even though it's all of 20 degrees with a windchill of zero or less. I'll go see the bull, who I've dubbed Eddie for no particular reason.

Coming around a curve, very slowly because the road is solid ice, I see Eddie's big blackness standing like a dark shadow, cold air blowing from nostrils as big as my hand.

I slow down, passing only a few feet from his immense deep set eyes. He seems to have a look of resignation on his dark curly face, as if he's tired of winter, though technically, it's just starting.

Eddie a ways behind us, my Blue Heeler, Weezee, and I walk along the road. The bull came through here earlier, and his hoofprints easily swallow mine. Weezee's paws could fit eight or ten to one of his, and she sticks her nose into the frozen cloven prints pushed deep into frozen mud and snow. She snorts, takes off chasing a flock of some kind of little gray birds wheeling low across the snowy flats. The other dogs refused to come along, wanting only to snooze by the fire.

I crunch along, keeping an eye on Eddie, his dark mass easily visible against the white snow—but he seems to like his spot on up the road. Weezee soon gives up on the birds, following at my heels, looking cold.

Neither of us lasts very long, and back in the warmth of my truck, we head home, where we get warm with Cassie and Moki next to the flickering light of the gas fireplace. It's cranked as high as it will go, and I still feel cold air coming in from somewhere.

Weezee is soon dreaming, legs moving like she's chasing something, maybe Eddie, if she's feeling brave.

I think of my time here in the desert, of my lost past, my tenuous future, then of this, the shortest day of the year.

The Farmer's Almanac says the actual solstice takes place at 1:08 a.m., so I try to stay up to feel the earth's axis grind to a slow halt and begin to tilt back the other direction, but I'm soon asleep, dreaming of Eddie, black as night, his massive body outlined against red and violet and purple and burgundy Aurora Borealis streamers that streak across the desert sky.

Eddie sighs as the earth tilts with the promise of spring and sweet desert clover, then paws the snow with his immense cloven hooves as the night grows shorter.

And as the earth tilts, so does my life, soon to be going in a different direction, though the change is as silent as this quiet winter solstice night.

DROWNED HOLE DRAW

It's early March, and I park my pickup where the faint road ends and start hiking west towards where the land tips precariously into a series of deeply incised draws. Pick one, any one, they all lead to the same place, into Drowned Hole Draw, which then drops a very straight 600 feet into the Black Box of the San Rafael River.

As I walk along, I think of a cattle rancher I met not too long ago in Green River. I didn't quite get his name, but he works in the winter helping maintain that big sweep of highway from the Colorado State Line to Ghost Rock at the top of the Swell.

The day I met him, he was in the coffee shop with his little five-year-old granddaughter, showing everyone a sketch she'd made of her pet rooster.

The little tow-headed girl reminded me of some of the kids I'd known in the city, the kind that go to schools like Carden and Montessori and have hired clowns at parties for their birthdays, but she instead had a pet rooster named Bobbie and lived in Green River, Utah.

Her grandpa was obviously very proud of her and beamed while everyone made over her sketch, which was actually a pretty good rendition. He just laughed and shook his head at the idea of a pet rooster.

Finally, he grabbed her up onto his shoulders, saying, "Let's go feed," and then put her into the back of his old pickup. This was a little joke he was playing on her, and she made sure he knew it wasn't where she intended to ride.

She was soon safely in the cab. One doesn't carry a treasure like that just anywhere.

Why do some struggle so long while others seem to know exactly who they are and where they belong?

I came out here once before, here to Drowned Hole Draw, with the man I loved, a man I thought might be like that Green River rancher—self-sufficient, strong, and gentle.

I was wrong.

The trail now narrows and drops deep into the canyon.

Walk quietly, so you don't scare the bighorn away, walk quietly like the mountain lion. Walk quietly, so you don't scare that dream away, the dream of the man you loved, lost in his anger. Walk quietly, so you can hear the flash-flood coming.

Walk quietly and listen to the soft sound of a young girl laughing, far in the distance, way over in Green River, sheltered by her grandfather's love and a pet rooster named Bobbie.

A STEADY COLD WIND BEARING RAVENS

Mid-April, and the winds are howling like hounds from Hell.

It was 74 degrees two days ago, a beautiful spring day with apricot trees and flowering plums in bloom against a backdrop of deep-blue sky. But today we've reverted to what seems like the precursor of Armageddon, huge thick cottonwood branches bending and twisting, trying to hold onto their early half-opened buds.

The wind is howling through the very bones of this old house, and as I look outside, the day becomes slowly darker from dust blown from who knows where, somewhere west—maybe from the top of the Swell, for it seems to have that yellow tint of Coconino sandstone. More likely, it's from the Oyster Shell Reef and adobe badlands that lie to the immediate west of town.

Tonight record colds are forecast, possibly down to 20 degrees. The dogs and I hunker down, feeling tired and listless all day, the dust and wind taking its toll on our ambition.

Looking out the window, I see four ravens flying into the wind, barely able to make headway, and I wonder why they're out flying in this at all. Maybe they started out in

Nevada and are being pushed backwards. They may end up in Colorado before the day is done—Colorado, where I hear they're having unseasonably early wildfires from a wet winter and dry March.

A steady cold wind bearing ravens and wildfires. It's that kind of wind.

We go out the River Road, and as I pass under the freeway, I notice something new—metal panels forming a corral leading into a loading chute.

Then I know.

John, the rancher, told me May was when they moved the cattle to the high country—Eddie's gone. Could it be?

I scan the countryside for the dark forms of Eddie and his companions, the other bulls he ranges with when he wants company. Six or eight of them, they're always around, and I can usually spot them pretty easily, ranging, roaming, eating, watching as we drive by, unblinking, un-afraid. Big bulls with their quite obvious bullness.

No Eddie. We drop down into the Morrison badlands and get out at our usual spot, wander through wind that feels even gustier and colder. Record lows are being set further west, and rain and snow are forecast for the Swell, which means we'll get the chill and possibly a few rain-drops down here on the desert.

I kick around, the dogs running and sniffing and being dogs, and then I find it—a huge piece of dino bone, easily weighing 10 pounds, beautiful gem quality, with cellular structures of red, yellow, and blue. Beautiful. Even the now-brutal wind can't blow away my elation.

I think of the thunder lizard whose bone I now hold in my hand, of what species it was, what it died from, how long ago, many mysteries. I carefully put it in a place where I can come back and enjoy it again.

We head back for the car, wind singing in my ears, singing songs of faraway places now brought here. Wind-sick, there's so much dirt in the air I can't even make out the Reef, a mere 20 miles away.

On the way back, I think of Eddie and wonder if he's headed for the mountains, the Tavaputs Plateau with its green bunchgrasses and wildflowers, or if he's headed to market.

I feel sad. Eddie's gone, and it marks the beginning of the season of heat, even though it feels cold now. But there's more—I feel that passing of time, of seasons, of impermanence. Time marked by Eddie is gone, marked by his footprints sunk deep in Mancos adobe clay. I miss Eddie.

How can one miss a free-ranging half-wild Angus bull? But I do.

Almost back to the underpass, I see something dark—a large bush, I think, one I've never noticed before. But as we get closer, I hold my breath—could it be?

Yes, it's Eddie, and nearby are his buddies, all peacefully grazing on that elusive desert forage (tiny desert clover, John tells me, that makes them some of the fattest bulls you can buy).

We pass slowly, savoring the long strong gaze from the curly face, the massive power of pure force that only a desert bull radiates. Ah, Eddie.

But the corral panels remind me that this may be Eddie's last day here in the desert. Something's definitely up.

We'll take one more day, whatever we can. Winds blow, rock and rattle the truck. Eddie stands, unshaken and seemingly oblivious. Surely he can see the panels and knows.

That we could all just savor the day, live for the day, like a big Angus bull named Eddie.

BULLISH DREAMS

Stockdogs and cowboys on horses, moving Eddie and his friends towards the corral. A large cattle truck waits nearby. We pass on. By the time we come back, they're gone.

Somehow I feel bad for Eddie, but maybe it's just personification. But no, I know Eddie will miss the freedom of the desert, no matter where he ends up.

Eddie came to me last night in a dream. He scared the bejeebers out of me, staring at me through a big crack in the door, trying to get in, his breath pushing through, warm on my face. I woke up afraid and couldn't go back to sleep.

I decided to write the dream down for future reference, as it's not often that I dream about big Angus bulls out to get me. They're not generally on my list of things to fear, like bears.

Hours later, when I woke again, I hadn't forgotten the dream. I lay there awhile, reliving it, feeling that warm breath punching in through the door, those intense eyes watching me, and the fear returned.

I started talking to Eddie, as I knew I had to calm him (or myself) down somehow, even though he seemed to exist only in my imagination. As far as I knew, the real Eddie was long gone in that cattle truck, either to mountain pasture or to a sales barn.

"Eddie," I entreated, "What's up? I passed you lots of times all winter, and all you did was raise your head and watch as we drove by. You didn't seem to mean me any harm then, so why now? I didn't have anything to do with you having to leave the desert. It wasn't my doing. I know you must miss it."

The bull softened a bit, but was silent. The stiff curls on his big forehead seemed even stiffer. His snorting was labored. I was about to give up on understanding the dream and go make myself a cup of coffee when Eddie finally spoke.

"I'm Eddie, the Angus bull. I'm powerful and scary."

I replied patiently, "I know, Eddie, I know. You scared me from a deep sleep last night. Why?"

Eddie snorted, "You've been ignoring me. I wanted to get your attention."

"It worked. But how can I be ignoring you when you're gone?"

"I'm still here. I'm Eddie the big bull that you wrote about. I'm angry with you because you hide from me and won't finish my story."

It was all starting to feel unreal, like I'd joined Eddie in the dream.

"I don't know the rest of your story, Eddie, you just disappeared on me. And I didn't know bulls spoke with such formality."

Eddie ignored my comment, continued, "You're wrong. I'm still around. I'm part of you. I'm your determination and power and strength. I'm your creativity. You hide from me and think you're safe, but I can find you. You fear me and try to run away from me. You fear me because you can't control me. I'm your wild and free life."

Eddie now seems softer, almost sad. He finishes, "You'll remain stuck here, ineffectual, until you let me in." He pauses, "But then I will let you ride my shoulders. You can hold onto the scruff on my big thick neck, and I'll take you all over the desert, show you places only big Angus bulls know."

With that, Eddie's gone.

"I'll be darned," I whisper to myself. I've never been much of one for dream analysis, but maybe I underestimate myself, maybe I can finish something for once, maybe I don't need to so carefully whittle my creativity, it'll come along on its own.

I laugh and the dogs come in to see if I'm OK. Tails wagging, they jump on me, half-knocking my breath out.

I close my eyes for a moment and picture Eddie standing again outside the door, looking in through the crack. He now wears a somewhat sheepish and gentle look for a giant Angus bull.

"OK, Eddie," I say. "OK, I'll write your story, but you have to keep your end of the promise. I want to see those secret places."

I think I hear a soft snort, but it's probably just Weezee wanting her breakfast.

GOING, ALWAYS GOING

The crabapple and pear trees in the park across the street bloom burgundy and white, framing the tall sleek Athena missile waiting for liftoff, nose pointing towards desert stars at night, desert sun by day. When the moon's full, as it is tonight, moonlight glints across its metal surface, melting along the long thin tall body of wrapped aluminum.

I'm slowly packing, filling boxes with my meager possessions—books, petrified wood, fragments of dinosaur bone, colorful rocks. When I'm done, it will all fit easily in my camper, along with dogs and camping gear.

Time to go. My rented bungalow has fallen into hard times, foreclosure. My rent apparently wasn't used to pay the mortgage.

It's mid-May, and the desert heat has been coming on for a while now, since that fierce wind two weeks ago, days of 70 and now 80 degree heat. In summer, the desert becomes a mirage-like dream, an illusion behind distant shimmering heatwaves of disconsolation. Summer is coming, when I long and pine for the desert from my cool mountain stronghold of cobalt-blue columbine and sweet-green aspen.

In fact, I'm already pining, not wanting to go, revisiting places I hold to in winter as if I'll never return, cherishing the sweeping vista of the San Rafael Reef, the banded candy-cane striped hills of Morrison Formation, the softer blue hills of adobe where boots sink and leave tracks for months or until the next big winds.

But I'm also craving home, I want to go home, back to the Colorado mountains of my youth, back to those high white-streaked blue peaks that melt into indigo sky with insolence.

Home, where my cousins Janie and Davie would come visit from Alaska, telling me tales of ice and bears, leaving a wake of farawayness when they would leave.

Back to Colorado, and when I'm there, I know I'll gaze into the dusty distance that holds my beloved desert and want to go back, to go home.

Cognitive dissonance. Lives filled with yearning, craving home, that place we can never truly be. My mom once said it's a natural yearning for a better place.

John the rancher stops by, telling me that Eddie brought 10 cents a pound more than any of the other bulls.

I'm reminded of a quote from Emerson, "Trust men, and they will be true to you." Eddie might beg to differ, if bulls could beg.

So, truck loaded, dogs panting, ready to go, I take one long last look at the tall thin spire of the Mormon Church across the street, turn and take in the serrated skyline of the Books, breathe in desert sun, desert dust, desert happiness.

I'm going back home. The Athena will guard things here while I'm gone, waiting for my hopeful return—but unbeknownst to me, I won't be back for a very long time.

PART II

AT ALTITUDE

Ouray Valley, Colorado

TWO RIVERS

It begins when you're not watching. You stop, look out at the big peaks, and all is well, blue sky mirroring the deeper blue of mountains laced with fingers of white snow, huge canvasses filled with winter's memory. Too much snow for July, you think, then go back to whatever's at hand.

But, before long, that deep survival mechanism that lies within all of us, descended from primitive times, wakes, tells you in a soft voice to pay attention, something's up.

You lift your eyes and look again—clouds have collected over the peaks so quickly you're in wonder, a thick white mass with an internal billowing so massive it makes their edges hang heavy, mammatic, drooping.

The storm begins.

You watch, storm drifting from south to southwest, defying desert logic, where storms track from west to east. But here, the massive uplifts make their own patterns, visible patterns in the retina of blue and white, invisible patterns in the sky of gravity and current.

All is well, lightning and tree-cracking thunder sailing on past to the southwest. You marvel at how thick the bolts of lightning seem, even though so far away, blazing wide like streaks of bright yellow-white paint from some land-

scape painter's brushstroke—maybe made when distract-
ed, some bolts zigzagging, some twisting and curling, some
thundering straight to ground with deadly intention.

But look! Now a new arm of the storm has crested from
behind the Cimarrons, stealthily bubbling through sky,
streaks of black rain shot through by more huge bolts.

And you rejoice, for it's been so long since you've seen
this, it's a shadow memory. Rain, sweet rain, sweet sweet
rain. It's been years since I've seen this mountain rain, rain
scented with pine and distant alpine meadows, cool, and
nothing like the torrential rains of desert flashfloods, those
rains of Noah. These sweet rains pass quickly, rumbling
their way on through, followed by the calls of some yellow-
breasted bird never known to desert heat and mirage.

And these mountain rains, they dance a song of winter, they remind you of how short these summers are, and
they tell you to prepare wisely, for soon they will change to
snow. Perhaps it's snowing on the big peaks this very moment, they whisper, get your wood, be ready. The ants, the
pikas, the squirrels, they hear this message, and they take
heed.

But before then, I will run back away to the desert, to
the comfort of drylands, where I will watch the mountains in the far distance as they whiten with winter. Will
the meadows here think of me when the soft white winds
come through?

The test of one's true love for a place is to ask where
you wish your ashes to be strewn, where you wish them to
be forever.

The desert. Bury me not on the lone prairie, bury me not on the lone alpine tundra, bury me on the lone desert, my home, where my heart tugs for succor, for freedom.

But now, as if to put to rest any notion that desert flash-flood rain can be more difficult, the rain has set in, become a hard drizzle, abandoned by lightning and thunder to the mundane.

I close the windows of the rented log cabin and marvel at how cool it is, knowing full well the desert at this very moment is terribly hot and teeming with millions of tiny gnats, each longing for a meal of blood—my blood.

I climb into the loft where I can see to the northwest, to my beloved desert, and yes, I can see a spot of sunshine. My beloved desert would never betray me, it's constant and unchanging, its heat barrier keeping rain away like Hadrian's Wall kept my crazy ancestor Scots from attacking the Romans.

Mid-July, we begin the monsoon season here in the San Juan Mountains, and these afternoon rains become more predictable, their lightning taunting those who dare to climb the big peaks. Some are more than taunted, are struck, returning down mountain flanks in litters carried by the living, for the peaks of the San Juans hold inordinate amounts of lightening-attracting iron.

THE IMPOSSIBILITY OF LONELINESS

I have a plastic toy dinosaur on my dash that reminds me of Bone Hill over by Green River, Utah, a different world, indeed, from this mountain stronghold where I currently live, near Ouray, Colorado.

Why is the dinosaur on my dash? I bought it in the little Melon Vine grocery store in Green River, where for some reason or other it struck my fancy, an impulse purchase.

Unplanned, it has played a somewhat sadistic role in the training of Moki, an Australian Shepherd-Blue Heeler who spent her first year of life in a cage in a shelter in California and is now with me, learning things most dogs learn as puppies.

It moves its legs and arms and makes weird screeching noises when I push the button on its stomach, and I accidentally found out that Moki is deathly afraid of the toy.

So, before I discontinued its use, the dinosaur came in handy anytime Moki decided to jump in the front seat without invitation, bark madly, or do anything else I deemed inappropriate. I would just grab the toy, push the button, and Moki would disappear into the back of my pickup, wiggling herself through the back window and into the camper shell.

I eventually started to feel guilty and tried to play with her, using the dinosaur as a sort of chewable toy, but even though she got to where she'd nibble on it, she never got into it much, always a bit nervous.

Now, even though the little dinosaur has outlived its usefulness as a dog-training tool, it still rides on my dash, reminding me of Bone Hill, reminding me that the Wild exists out there in that wonderful candy-cane Brushy Basin member of the Morrison Formation near Green River.

I need to remember that, and often, for I need the Wild, even if just in memory. I think we all do, but most have forgotten what it is they need, some indefinable mysterious tugging that they try to avoid or ignore, or maybe even search for and seldom find, seeing how it's so far away and perhaps even frightening.

It's really just that big mountain over there, that hard-scrabble juniper so twisted and stunted it's become like a bonsai, that little quiet stream hidden by the buckbrush— all a part of us, braided into the very strands of our DNA, blazed into our ancient memory.

Sometimes, I can imagine the little dinosaur (a T-Rex with lots of big plastic teeth) asking me, "What do you think about when you find my bones out in the Morrison, solid as rock because they are rock, petrified, laced with blues and reds?"

Once, out in the desert, very alone, I began to feel lonely, a rare thing, as I lay stretched out on the slickrock, mourning the people lost to me through death, distance, and the passage of time.

It was hot, over 100 degrees, and a large juniper sheltered me from the sun, as much as you can be sheltered when the entire atmosphere feels like it's burning up.

Maybe it was from the heat, but I began to feel as if I were part of a vast continuum of molecules, one that connected everything to itself, to each other, encircling the Earth and then spreading out to the distant stars.

It suddenly occurred to me how preposterous it was to think that I was alone while surrounded by such trees, alive in their own right, citizens of a different order, but still very alive, radiating out their lifeness in the desert heat. I was humbled and awestruck by the thought.

What price are we willing to pay to be part of the Wild, to return to our ancient home of rock and star and juniper? The Wild is in our genetic makeup, but in order to find it for ourselves, we have to be willing to be alone out there with the junipers, alone out in those places where we're not really alone.

And so, in a way, it's impossible to be alone, as we're always surrounded by life—and yet, as humans, we do get lonely, and it's an impossibly difficult thing.

Do you dream of polar bears dancing along the Aurora Borealis? Can you feel the amazing presence of the forest around you in the deep night, even though you're inside a house, alone?

If not, why not?

MAY THE WOLF BE WITH YOU

My neighbors, good people that they are, have invited me to a dinner party, just a small affair with another couple they're good friends with. Their friends have a website that distributes strange and weird tidbits and stories to various newspapers, and they make a good living at it. It strikes me as a bit strange and weird.

There will be stir fry for dinner, they say, and yes, jello, since they're Mormons, originally from Utah.

I laugh—they know I've just come from Utah and am not Mormon and are making a little joke on themselves and the potlucks the close-knit Mormons seem to always be having that invariably include variations on the jello theme.

"Sure, I'll come," I say, all the while an inner voice mocking my attempt to be sociable with, "You'll be sorry."

I try. I actually even look forward a bit to the human contact, to getting to know my kind neighbors a little better. Eventually, the day of the dinner (or the reckoning, if you prefer), I come to my senses, realizing I will indeed be sorry if I attend, and I wander over to their house an hour early and knock on the door, my intention being to beg off with some lame conjured excuse about someone needing me somewhere for something unexpectedly. Such excuses to avoid human gatherings have come naturally to me all my life. I've eventually learned to heed the advice to "know thyself," as I've had a 99% failure rate at enjoying such things.

I'm invited in and, not wanting to be rude, I go inside to explain my case, which they kindly accept and generously express regrets for, offering me jello to take home.

The house is beautiful, custom designed by the middle-aged couple, she an oil painter and he a computer engineer who telecommutes. It's over-decorated for my taste, cutesy country with little stuffed ducks and frilly curtains and overstuffed furniture, but it's their house, not mine, so I enjoy it in a detached way.

The entry opens into the living room, with a special alcove that holds an open Book of Mormon on a stand with a picture of the Mormon Temple in Salt Lake City hanging above.

Along the wall of the living room is a large organ, complete with what seems like hundreds of stops and pedals and bells and whistles, all set in an ornate carved oak case with ivory keys.

I smell stir-fry pork cooking in the kitchen. To me, eating pork seems like eating dogs might seem, as pigs are smarter than dogs, so they say. I'm glad to not be staying and eating pork.

The house is warm and cozy, and the whole place smacks of security and comfort and of the keeping out of wolves—actually, more like totally forgetting that wolves even exist.

Before I know it, the engineer, who plays for the local church services and informs me in a modest way that he's actually even played the huge organ at the temple in Salt Lake, is playing that perennial Mormon favorite, "Oh Come All Ye Saints," pulling out all the stops, while I dutifully sit on a large couch upholstered in a dark green with autumn leaves splashed everywhere in a myriad of golds and reds, sipping hot chocolate.

For just a brief moment, I want to go Mormon. Kind of the opposite of a captured coyote wanting to go feral, I want to embrace such stability and comfort and tradition and security.

But I eventually escape, go feral, running like a wild coyote, knowing deep inside the price is too high. Freedom beckons, and I cross through the evening light to my cabin, locking the door behind me for a moment, as if I were being followed.

Such nice people—why do I feel like this? I open the back door, dogs following, and we all head up the trail behind the house, climbing up and up into a wild country of thick scrub oak and quaking aspen, a forgotten animal trail going into places people seldom go.

We stop only when we can no longer see anything to do with houses. The dogs snuff around, and I sigh that sigh one can sigh only after a narrow escape. I cuss blueblazes, just to quell the spell of it all, then end up in the deep wild bluestem grass in laughter at the irony. Close call.

The sun begins to set behind the ridge, casting its own spell, bringing me back to my senses, leaving only a trace of regret.

Now, the alpenglow begins. Melting upwards, the big peaks' iridescent blues begin to change spectrum, become bold with sunrays, changing into pinks, purples, and deep burgundies. The closer peaks fade into shadow—Chimney Rock, Courthouse, Turret Ridge—then earth's shadow climbs the steep slopes of Dunsinane, finally topping out on Coxcomb, and at last, the wild and airy slopes of Wetterhorn.

Radiance now faded, gone into gray, most of the birds and wild things follow into their deep evening slumber, that time when tawny cougars awaken, stretch, and see the world at their feet. Deep shadows embrace the big cats as well as the big peaks, and my admiration embraces cougarness, fierceness, lone independence, elusive like the great cats sleeping in their strongholds. The purity of the big peaks surrounds all, all bold hearts, a purity I long for and could die for.

Alpenglow lingers a long time, and I see sunset far away, in my memory, in the Utah desert, on endless seas of sandstone fins and whalebacks, glowing red in oblique light. Then my mind drifts to the gray Bookcliffs, now gold with sunlight, then on westward to the notch on the San Rafael Reef skyline, where the sun is now setting a full 15 minutes after setting here in the San Juans, intense, with just a glimpse of the green flash.

With so many wild places to treasure, how can one measure which is loved most?

I now stumble back towards the house, glad for the white spots on the dogs, dim beacons to follow in the darkness. I can see the glowing windows of my neighbors' house, light spilling out like golden jello from an overfilled plate complete with every delicacy one could ever want, inviting one to come, come be a Saint, find happiness and security here, here in the works of Man.

Now home, I feed the dogs, then cook a tofu dog on a willow stick over the gas flames on the little stove, burning it, like I always do without intending to, then stuff the hot-dog into a bun, adding some mustard. I go outside and eat, sitting on the deck, where I can now hear the faint strains of another dirge-like hymn drifting from the neighbors' windows as bats dodge through the darkness after insects.

And so, to forget the organ, I sing my own song, ever so quietly, an old tune from childhood:

Ah, the summertime is comin'
And the leaves are sweetly turning,
And the wild mountain thyme
Blooms across the purple heather
Will you come, laddie, come.

Somehow, it brings comfort. Stars unfold, layer after layer, stars unseen in the thicker desert air, stars seen only when one is close to Paradise.

After awhile, the stars are so thick that my mind becomes unsettled with the immensity, the perfection, so I shake off the night chill, go inside, close the windows, tuck in the dogs, wrap up in my down sleeping bag, and go to sleep.

Oh, and I leave the door cracked just enough to let the wolves in, should they wish to visit. Dinosaurs welcome, too, as long as Moki approves.

RIVER ONE: RED WATER

It's the end of July, that time when rivers return to sanity after the flows of spring—flows that drifted this year into June and July from the big snows.

I stand by the river and throw sticks out to the dogs, who jump in and retrieve with that frenzy reserved for labradors and other retrievers, though these guys haven't a drop of retriever blood, not that's apparent, anyway.

Once in awhile one gets out into the stronger current and has to swim, water now up to neck, eventually bowling out of current like a ball seeks the gutter.

Simple pleasures, not lost on desert dogs who rarely see water, yet alone get to play in it.

Water sparkles, a pale blue like the color of glacial ice, rippling and chattering along like the squirrels in nearby tall slender narrow-leaf cottonwoods, trees cousin to the big Fremont cottonwoods that inhabit the desert and bend to the ground with stored water. These mountain cottonwoods have no need to store something so plentiful here—rain, snow, river.

Moskies, mosquitoes, also inhabit the riverway, biting whoever whatever whenever in a frenzy less sentient than that of dog madly following stick in water.

No one seems to fish these waters, here below the little mountain town of Ouray, for such pale waters belie a high mineral content leaching from mines filled with heavy metals.

River water runs pale blue like towering mountains stand pale blue, topped with whipped-cream clouds in darker blue sky. Cottonwoods, box elder, willows, all wave happily in the breeze, green as chlorophyll can get.

Summers here are short, as are such things hinting of Paradise.

A trip into the high mountains a few days back brought notice of a few yellowing aspen, fresh snow on Whitehouse Mountain, snow now melted. The San Juans will be glaciated if next winter is as harsh as the last, for huge snowfields wait, refusing to let go and return to ocean, perhaps enjoying their lofty views of peaks and faraway red desert, taunting the heat.

Some snowfields bear a red tinge, desert sand blown many miles by storm to enjoy unlikely company.

This river, the Uncompahgre, is named after a band of Utes who inhabited this country, and the little town at the head of the valley is the namesake of Chief Ouray. I've been told Uncompahgre means "red water."

This small river amazes me at its size, draining so many mountains, yet nearly wadeable, even now, after an abnormally high runoff, snowbanks still melting in the high country. It's a happy river, even though tainted by toxic metals and mourning its loss of fish companionship.

If I put a message in a bottle, say an old Pepsi bottle from the 1960s like I found over at the missile range by

Green River, this little river would catch it up and the bottle would first journey 50 miles or so to the confluence with the Gunnison River in Delta, then another 60 miles or so to the mighty Colorado at Grand Junction, where all traces of big blue peaks would muddy into the reds that give the big river its Spanish name. The bottle would then course on down into the big desert canyons, eventually ending in the stagnant and dying Lake Powell.

And so is life, and each of us is floating along like that bottle, though our river is time. And unbeknownst to me and my cousin Davie, Janie is living her last summer, way over there on the big banks of the Pacific Ocean, on the beaches of Hawaii.

She will soon return to Alaska, and we'll all ask why and wish she hadn't.

RIVER TWO: GREEN WATER

Every day while still in the little town of Green River, the dogs and I would drive down to the bridge to check the river, my daily duty as river keeper, a self-appointed task to ensure I didn't forget that all is in flux.

That river was the Green, the mighty Sisk-a-dee-agie, Shoshone for "river of the prairie chicken," later corrupted to Seedskadee by the fur trappers and early settlers.

The mighty Green, draining water from the high peaks of Wyoming, the Wind River Range, melting snows with a brief journey through Colorado's dinosaur land to prepare for the big canyons of Desolation and Gray and Labyrinth and Stillwater, then on to the Colorado and high adventure through Cataract Canyon, an adventure that ends abruptly in the silt behind Glen Canyon Dam. There, if evaporation doesn't start a new journey, the waters run through spill-way on down into the mighty Gorge itself, the Grand Canyon.

Ah, such an amazing journey, one I'd be afraid to take, myself. And look, there, bobbing along, a bottle—quick, fish it in. Moki grabbed it in her teeth and brought it to me. She loves bottles, especially the plastic ones that water comes in—she throws them into the air and catches them, then chews them up.

It was capped, and inside was a message, just like in the movies.

Bert's Boat Repair, Flaming Gorge, 435-784-3445

I smiled and threw the bottle back in. It was quickly gone, floating on down the river.

A strong will is like the river, running straight and true, single-minded, and nothing can stop it, for better or worse. Like the river needs water to be a river, one needs optimism to replenish their life's journey. Our emotions can be complex, a detailed map of our history, a map we can study and try to understand so it will lead us to better places.

We must study the map and know where we came from to know where we can go. Like the river, our lives can flow free, or we can end up behind a damn dam.

And so, here we are, only a short time after studying the Green, me and the dogs, throwing sticks into this mountain river, the Uncompahgre. Sticks are never returned, but captured with wild Olympic-type lunges, then released to go on down into the deeper currents.

I did recognize one particularly twisted stick as we crossed the bridge a few miles downstream on our way home, it floating away to the mighty adventures of new currents, never to return, kind of like a small boat on the river of life—or the river of no-return, however you choose to look at it.

For Janie, it was the river of no-return, and I found out later she wanted it that way.

RIVER THREE: BEAR WATER

The river's now in the throes of summer, sedate and lazy. I tire of throwing sticks, especially since I have to find new ones each time and the shore is now bereft of them. Sometimes, the dogs grab their own stick from the far shore and chase it into the water.

The water sparkles, dances, and later, my river photos show an odd golden glint from the heavy metals—this is silver and gold country.

The valley is lush and green from the frequent thunderstorms, one of which is now beginning to push over the shoulders of the Magic Carpet. The doe I saw yesterday was up to her ears, literally, in grass.

Kaboom, storm warns, dogs flee water for car.

But all in all, it's only a light sprinkle accompanied by more lightning and thunder.

We sit for a moment, river water nearby, sky water on windshield.

Dogs whoof. I've never heard this sound from them before—it's not a growl, not a bark, but a whoof, a warning. Ears alert. Eyes big.

A black bear! On all fours, coming up from the river, where it must've been drinking.

Was it there all along, watching us play? Bears play.

I think of a friend in Montana and her close bear encounter that pulled scalp back and left curly marks on her face like corkscrew lightning. Surgery fixed her scalp and removed most of the marks, but nothing can remove bear claws slicing through dreams, except courage.

Bear is now loping through meadow, and I've managed to take a few photos. Bear pauses, turns, and I think I sense a kindred spirit—playful, yet potentially dangerous, as are many humans.

Brain mapping shows that we feel the greatest sense of elation and even happiness when dealing with events of great challenge and danger. Are bears the same?

They never captured the bear that harmed my friend. She's glad about that. She reports that some of her so-called friends did her greater harm than the bear by betraying her confidence to what she called the ghoulish press.

At least bears are straightforward and honest—and bears know how to play—except the one that killed Janie wasn't playing at all.

QUEEN ANN'S LACE

No dreams come during the night, nothing, just a blackness of lost time that only the stars hanging overhead understand.

I slowly wake, as if on a drifting boat slipping from some dark shadowy lake into muted daylight.

Something's wrong.

I'm awake now, and I know my sleep is complete, but it seems too early, as if waking to a full moon instead of sunlight.

Throwing off the warm comforter, I get up and stumble to the window, pulling back the curtain.

Fog.

The thick forest is draped in gray, and I can barely make out the cliffs above. Thick mist fills the valley below like an amorphous presence, slowly drifting downwards, damp and almost prescient.

And now I can hear a soft patter on the roof as the rains begin. I close the curtain, which clings to the window glass. Rains now earnest, coming down so hard it makes the slender aspen leaves turn and twist on their stems, making the trees appear to shimmer.

Rain, yet more rain.

I now long for the distant desert, my home. The aspen forest here is lush, thick with blue lupine and white daisies and Queen Ann's lace, with yellow aster and the blues of tall grasses. Blurs of distant yellow mark where skunk cabbage turns much too early. Waist-high mullein whispers that an early winter hides behind Orion's belt.

Rain lifts. Fog paces up and down the valley, not sure where to go. Now it pulls back enough to reveal the vibrant green leaves of the happy aspens, their white bark now yellow in the dim light.

I freely gave all this up—the beauty, the cool summer air, the long inviting blue-green slopes that remind me of Scotland, land of my mother's dreams.

No one made me leave this place of my own birth. It seems a shame that all this beauty is lost on me, and I'm well aware that many would gladly trade places with me, to be here in the midst of this serenity, rain or no.

I know I should be happy to be here, and in a way I am. I have many happy memories here—hiking alone on the animal trails, once stopping to watch a young black bear playing, unaware of my presence, memories of seeing incredible sunrises and sunsets, shooting stars, moonlight glowing on white aspen bark as if lit from within, memories of fields of wildflowers that look like a Monet painting.

And yet, for all its alpine beauty, there's always an undercurrent here, like the electricity that fills the air right before the massive lightning bolts sear through, making aspen leaves tremble in fear.

That undercurrent speaks of an infinite unhappiness deep within, a craving for the wide spaces and distant horizons of the desert, its emptiness and barrenness and desolation and freedom.

These mountains, for all their beauty, are places of restrictions, closed in and claustrophobic, where one can't see out without climbing.

But there's more to it than that. The mountains are a place of great restriction, but the desert is a place of great prediction—you can see the big storms coming in, unlike the mountains, where they just spring up, catching you unawares. And in the desert, you can see dust devils coming, something you don't see in the mountains at all.

Yet, there's even more than this. The desert is a place of great distances, distances that make you feel content to see them and know they're there. One can see these mountain ranges far far away and know what they hold—fogs and mists and alpenglow and aspen leaves happily spinning in the rain.

Shade your eyes and look into that far blue distance at these ridges and peaks and misty haze, and you know all is well here. Dream through the balmy desert nights, sleeping well in that knowledge.

In the desert, sun lingers forever, rays lighting up these distant mountains with a pink alpenglow that makes one's heart glad for the seeing.

I want to be back down there right now instead of up here in the deep chill, even though it's 100 degrees there, too hot to return, even though the yearning's an illness only the desert can heal.

And now look! The light changes—sun breaks through thick gray clouds for but a moment, reminding the world it can disperse the fog and rain anytime it wishes. It then quickly retreats after seeing how the world is faring without it, returning to the desert where it blazes down, unimpeded by forest and fog and rain, happy in its shadowmaking.

A chill follows the closing clouds. The ruby red cliffs of Utah call my name without speaking.

A breeze catches the trees, flinging drops of water from wet leaves. Nearby are two gnarled aspens, old, trunks twisted together, black barren branches protruding out. They're tall and graceful in spite of their strangeness, with a thick canopy of leaves high above.

Fog rolls down the valley as if leaving, but is soon back, thick white tendrils engulfing entire trees in a heartbeat, moving fast. It soon engulfs me in a dreamlike state, and I know it's time to go. Where, I don't know, but I quickly prepare to leave my rented mountain cabin. I have no choice, anyway, as it's been sold. Always time to go, again and again.

It doesn't take long to throw everything into my pickup. One last look around this mountain paradise, as sun comes out for a brief goodbye, lighting golden aster like small searchlights.

I feel a pang of what could have been here, like a dream that won't come true.

My dad, the tall blue-eyed man with the shock of red hair and an intelligence like mountain lightning—he would've been content here. His happiness rested under the jagged volcanic gaze of the Cimarron ridge, nestled in the mountains, just like here. To him, the mountains were home.

But all I ever do when not in the desert is plot how to get back, and I somehow feel like I'm betraying him, even perhaps betraying myself, always fleeing back to the desert, where life is easier in some ways and harder in others.

I stand for a moment in the silence as the trees stand still, fog now at my feet. I've heard very little sound here for days—coyotes once, and one afternoon was filled with the majestic and fatal sound of lightning strikes and thunder—but otherwise, the forest has been totally silent. I did hear a woodpecker late one evening hammering a distant tree.

I'm restless, like the fog, and I finally get the dogs into the truck, starting it and driving away, my lonely cabin now happy in its regained solitude, enveloped by thick clouds.

The rain returns to bid me farewell, making it hard to see the muddy road that crawls down the mountain. Windshield wipers beat back and forth, trying to whisk water away.

Suddenly, all is silent, and I realize the rain has retreated back up the mountain, finally letting us go.

I feel happy now for the going, and a beam of sunlight breaks through clouds in my rear-view mirror, lighting the aspen, turning their bark from yellow to a blazing white, as they should be.

The road begins to dry out, and soon I'm down in the valley, following the creek. I look back to clouds parted and high summits bathed in gold.

Soon, while I'm in the warmth of the desert, it will be snowing on the loftiest of them all.

PART III

I DREAM OF BEARS

Utah and Colorado

THAT THIN SPACE
OF EXISTENCE

It's nearing the end of monsoon season, and all I can do is wait for each storm to travel on through.

Sometimes they take their time—those are the long ones, the tank rains, the ones that remind you of how finite you are, that try your patience. They roll in, roll around, and sometimes roll you over.

Today's storm is like that. It's brought flash-floods to the canyons of Zion, those mighty fierce and deep winding canyons. It's coming this way, to wash out the canyons here in this part of Utah, to cleanse them of summer heat and smoke.

I start coffee in my little pan over my one-burner propane stove, wondering if I can finish the job before the rains come. The huge monoliths, Merrimac and Monitor, glow orange in the strange light cast by the black clouds that filter sunlight like a coffee filter. They wait, wondering if waters will bring new rockfall, altering their sheer faces, bringing them closer to melting into the sandy flats.

A rock in the near distance looks like a small round house, complete with windows, and I decide to go investigate. Just then, Moki barks, and Cassie jumps. I see nothing.

Coffee cup in hand, I walk to the rock, which holds packrat nests. Cactus flourishes from cattle overgrazing, the sad story here, the native plants now part of someone's hamburger.

Now I see them—fresh deer tracks, only minutes old. A lone deer just came through, making Moki bark.

Clouds darken, twist, roll, cluster together with a black madness, then turn a deep dangerous-looking steel-blue. A real gully washer is brewing.

Worried, I gather the dogs and walk back to the truck, but by then the clouds have already moved to the northwest, directly over Monitor, where they unleash lightning, then just as quickly pass on, raining on the green oxidized-iron slopes of Garden Mesa.

I drive up where I can better see out and am greeted by a black mass of clouds looming to the west, moving in fast, the entire length of the horizon, stretching from Temple Mountain in the southern San Rafael Reef to the La Sals.

Trouble tonight.

I decide to shelter under one of the large picnic lean-tos at Lone Mesa Campground, since no one's there. I wait until it's nearly dark to set up camp, leaving my options open. Always good to leave one's options open.

I pull the picnic table from under the shelter, making room to back my truck partly under the large roof. The ground is wet. Either the shelter leaks or it's recently rained so hard the water came in sideways.

I find out later it leaks.

By dusk, I can see the distant La Sal Mountains are banked with black clouds covered with white trim, like an old-fashioned winter coat, black boiled wool with white velveteen. Trouble over there tonight.

The campground is spread out, its sites meant for large groups, and soon a car comes and parks across the way. A man and teenaged boy get out and walk around under the shelter way over there. I know this because I have my binoculars.

I feel safer out in the backcountry where few humans range, and I rarely stay in campgrounds. I'm here only for the shelter.

I finally set up camp, putting up my little backpacking tent. It never takes long, but sometimes it feels difficult. Then I sit in my pickup and wait. It's too early to go to bed, and it's starting to sprinkle. The dogs cozy up in the back, bored.

Below, red-walled Bartlett Canyon stretches out as if to recline for the night, and I can see clear to Crescent Junction, where the lights of a train seem to move slowly into a distance of haze and cloud. A raven wings over me, checking everything out—whoosh whoosh whoosh.

The sky to the north is black with the storm that passed over Merrimac and Monitor, which has made its way clear to the Bookcliffs, seeing what havoc it can wreak there. The lights of the cars on the interstate twinkle, far away. I wonder where everyone's going.

And now it hits—like the waves of an immense whirlpool in the North Sea, it slams hard, unexpected. I reel, brace myself, taken unawares. The desolation, loneliness, has returned.

My defenses are better than they used to be, and I understand more now. I know there's a choice. I don't have to open the door to it, to this wanting to go home when you don't have one.

My new neighbors, way over there, have their tent up, and I can make out voices in the distance. Sometimes other people trigger it, reminding me of what I don't have.

I turn on the pickup radio, trying to stave the feeling away—classic country from Price, Utah, just over on the other side of the Big Empty, a good hundred miles away.

I have a pocket full of heartbreaks,

And I'm a thousand miles from home.

Guess I'm not the only one. Despair seems to be a human condition, though I usually find solace deep in the heartland of solitude, even when loneliness haunts me.

It's still sprinkling, and it's almost eight, so I crawl into the tent. Nothing better to do.

Soon I can see lightning flash through tent's nylon sides, and it's raining hard, pounding the metal roof of the shelter. I'm happy to have the shelter, as my tent won't leak and be soggy all night.

But I soon hear water sprinkling in on the tent. The shelter leaks. False sanctuaries.

I finally go to sleep, only to be awakened by new voices. Someone's come into the campground during the night, a man and woman. It's still raining hard, and I vaguely wonder if the ground under the shelter will flood. I drift back to sleep.

Something's wrong, the ground's all tilted, and I keep drifting to one side, Cassie smack on top of me. I finally get up and put her in the pickup with Moki. Weezee sleeps quietly by me, cozy in her down sleeping bag.

I shine my light around to assess the situation, but everything's OK. It's only one a.m. and seems like it should be dawn.

Long nights, winter's coming. There will be trouble here. Cold and snow. Ravens, prepare.

I wake again, water dripping into the tent as I contrast this with the ungodly heat and smoke of the past week. One extreme to another. I drift back to sleep, then wake again. I've been dreaming of Eddie the Bull. He's happily grazing by the road, but when he sees me, he turns into a big black bear and lopes away.

It's now five a.m., the longest night. I get up, check on the dogs, then go back to bed, wake up at six, then get up and make coffee, even though it's still dark. The dogs are happy to sniff around.

Sun soon rises through mist and clouds, clouds too dense for much light to break through, and everything feels heavy and wet.

I watch as the eastern sky takes on a bit of red.

How does that old sailer's saying go? Red clouds at dawn, sailer begone? No, red clouds in morn, sailer be warned. In any case, we're in for more weather.

Weezee, Moki, and Cassie sit quietly on the picnic table, waiting for breakfast. I guess they figure they're closer to the food if they're on the table—to heck with people manners.

I sit back and sip my coffee, loneliness forgotten.

Another day in the desert. No place I'd rather be.

A CONSPIRACY
OF RAVENS

Winter lurks behind the mountains, and a cold wind blows from nowhere. It's late October.

I sit and wait. Where are the ravens? Have they abandoned me? Has this wind taken them to some foreign land, some mesa far on the other side of the rim, unseen, unknown? Is that where this wind is blowing from?

I've brought nuts today, high energy food. They'll need it. They'll come. Patience is all I have left.

They're here suddenly, scoop up the nuts, wing away, floating over sandstone fins, riding the currents together, a dance of two that makes me lonely. Their wings are burnished blue-black in the sun.

The next day, I'm up early to see the sunrise—but it doesn't rise. Cloud cover, light snow on and off. Sometimes when it's like this I see the ghosts—all those who passed through, animals and people alike. They float across the land like mist.

It's chilly and overcast. I hear ravens, far away in the distance, and now I see two blackish ghosts in the mist, floating across the big fins.

Suddenly, croak croak, they're here. A flock of ravens is called a conspiracy of ravens, but what do you call a pair? Unconditional love?

It's snowing way over on the San Rafael Reef—I can see the distant mists. Or are those just more ghosts?

Everything is very still, waiting for the storm. I hear voices. Winds pick up, time to go.

I find out later that this was the same day Janie died.

MT. SNEFFELS

The mountain's summit block stands against the sky, freed of stifling snow by helpful winds, and I soon sit on its highest point, lungs aching, heart breaking. I look to the west, where I can make out the curvature of the earth in the far hazy distance. I've come back to Colorado, but just for a brief time.

This peak in the Sneffels Range of the San Juan Mountains holds me some 14,158 feet above sea level, though the only sea nearby is the memory of the great Western Interior Seaway, a memory held in the gray Cretaceous shales in the valleys far below. That ancient sea was half a mile deep, 600 miles wide, and over 2,000 miles long.

Pondering deep geologic time while standing alone on a heady jagged peak on a short winter day makes one want to stop for a moment and ponder who you are, where you came from, and where you can go if you wish, assuming you're comfortable without any answers.

Otherwise, you begin to feel like you're high in a crow's nest, adrift at sea, eyes searching through the mists for a port, any port, to call home.

It's such times that thoughts of that distant desert—that one just over there at the place where the earth meets the sky and it all curves—well, such thoughts smooth the mind. And here, alone on this majestic terrifying peak in early November, I need all the consolation I can muster. I've stood here before, but never alone on the edge of winter.

I've come to spread my mom and dad's ashes from the very top of the mountain they both loved into the countryside they loved even more. I've come in early winter so I can be alone, timing it before the mountain is cloaked in deep snows and thereby impassible.

It was summer the last time we were all together—far below in a field of wild yellow mustard and purple aster edged by stands of fresh-leaved Gamble's oak.

And even though it's now winter, I imagine a warm breeze sifting up from that meadow, where leggy skunk cabbage edges a hillside shadowed by tall ponderosa pine—the meadow where we stood and gazed at this very peak, talking about what it would be like to be way up here.

My mom was a month older than my dad, and she died exactly a month before he did. It was like they'd both been set to the same timer.

I eat a half-frozen apple, my feet dangling into space, then take the two small boxes from my daypack. Sunlight plays through clouds, and I imagine I can see, far below, a lone ponderosa pine with a perfect circle of shade, like the circle of life.

Looking around, the scene is one of great beauty and terror, for I'm surrounded on three sides by endless rugged verticality, strange contorted spires and forms created by volcanic forces, peaks with names like Kismet and Potosi and Teakettle and Cirque, all towering from 12,000 to over 14,000 feet above sea level.

Now a hawk swings low, circles above me, low enough that I can see its tattered wings, one side with a feather missing. It reminds me of my mom, so beautiful, wanting her freedom, also tattered, an adventurer at heart caught in the domesticity of another era.

Fingers of last year's snow claw their way up the impassible cliffs of blue-gray tuft, and giant snowbanks top impossible slopes of tundra. White fluffy clouds catch on peaks, then break free in tattered scraggles, only to again merge into fullness.

I startle, thinking I see something from the corner of my eye. Is someone here? I'm irritated, wanting the summit to myself. I turn and for a brief moment imagine I see a magnificent polar bear, its white coat reflecting the crimson of the Aurora Borealis. Polar bears—the only bears that more often than not view humans as prey.

Wind swirls, there's nothing there.

The mountains turn deeper blues as clouds shift, the immense craggy tops silently speaking of their own presence. The stillness gets even stiller, and the air is hung with expectation, anticipation—of what—deep winter snows? Falling stars?

Now the ponderosa far below whispers in stirring breeze—don't forget me, me, me—remember me when you're far away over a horizon even I in my height can't see, far away in your desert warmth as I'm held by deep snows, sleeping, sleeping, waiting for your return.

I say nothing, for I know, deep in my heart, that I will never return.

The ashes are very light, and they take to the sky like birds released from a cage. I watch for awhile as breeze catches them, twirling them higher and higher over my head. Looking straight upwards, I can make out two faintly sparkling stars in the black vaulted sky.

I stand. Time to go.

And so, in peace, I leave, never to come again to this place, for nothing holds together, ashes to ashes, dust to dust.

But wait! Breeze again stirs, quick tumult, and all is separated, ashes flying away to eternity, to my desert over that curved horizon, where they will fall to earth and finally find rest in some redrock labyrinth of canyon, beneath pinyon pine, distant cousin of the Ponderosa.

And when I return to my desert home, ashes will finally arrive too, drifted on wind, my parents again with me as I was once with them, born of their conjoined love.

I make it down off the mountain by midnight, sliding down the steep endless scree field to the tundra, my headlamp lighting my way, then on down into Yankee Boy Basin, where my truck waits, cracked windshield bearing a dusting of snow.

By the time I'm down the narrow shelf road to the small town of Ouray, the streets are covered in glistening powder, street lights dim with falling flakes as big as white butterflies.

I know these kinds of mountain snows, they get big and deep. I should stop and hole up here, but I don't, instead driving on to the next town, Ridgway, then to the next and next until I'm finally at Davie's in Grand Junction, dogs happy to see me, snow but a memory as rain falls in this desert town.

I collapse on his couch, knowing in the morning I'll move on, head south, like the Canada geese flee the cold of the north.

Perhaps I can find a new place to call home, a place where the storms dissipate before they can even dream themselves into being.

THAT MELANCHOLIC DIVIDE

The news comes my very first night in southern Utah, the news that will divide my life into two parts: Pre-Bear and Post-Bear.

"You make it down south OK?" Davie asks.

"I'm camped at Snow Canyon. It's beautiful down here—most of the trees are still green," I answer.

I can tell something's wrong from the tautness of his voice. Is he in trouble again for drinking? He told me he'd quit.

There's a long pause, and I ask, "Davie, everything OK?"

I now hear a quiet sobbing. He finally gathers himself, answers, "Chin, it's Janie."

I suddenly feel cold. I'm on Sneffels again, wind cutting through me, looking towards that distant curved horizon, towards my beloved desert, feet entombed in blue ice, unable to move. The polar bear is back, watching me intently, no longer bothering to hide, predator studying prey.

"Chin, she's gone."

Now I've fallen off the cliffs and am spinning round and round, downward into an intense blizzard, snow choking me, unable to speak.

Davie repeats, "Chin, did you hear me? Janie's dead."

Somehow I've miraculously grabbed onto the branches of a big Ponderosa pine, holding fast against the wind, wondering how a Ponderosa could be growing this high on a mountain. I crawl into its deepest branches.

Finally, I ask, "What happened?"

"Chin, she decided to go back to Alaska. You know we were raised there, but she'd never shown any interest in returning other than a few days here and there once every few years. Apparently she decided to take a week off and go back. She was hiking in Chugach Park, and nobody knows for sure, but the authorities think she surprised a bear. It attacked her and mauled her."

"Was it a polar bear?" I ask.

"A polar bear? No, there aren't any polar bears in southern Alaska, as far as I know. It was a brown bear, a grizzly."

I now feel a sense of urgency, a panic. I reply, "I have to go up there."

"Chin, it's late fall. You know what it's like there. Roddie's flying to Anchorage from Hawaii. It's best to let him handle everything, since he's her son. There's nothing you can do. I can't go because I'm still on probation for my DUI and can't leave the state. I don't have the money, anyway. Roddie will take care of it."

"He'll need help," I answer, my throat now taut.

"His wife's going, too. They'll have Janie cremated and spread her ashes in Hawaii. I just wish she'd stayed there. She was too young."

I answer, "I'm going to go up there."

"Wait till spring. You can drive and take the dogs and stay as long as you want. OK, Chin?"

"I dunno, maybe."

And so, now back south again for the winter, a winter that suddenly feels it will have no end. Janie's gone. She was always my champion, the one I could call when I needed to talk, like a sister, though in reality my first cousin. Why hadn't she stayed in Hawaii? She loved it there. Why would she go back to Alaska? She always said she didn't like it there, and now she's gone—forever.

In shock, I have no choice but to carry on.

No bears here, where the trees are still green, some turning gold. The days are in the 60s and 70s, the nights cool but pleasant. I set up my tent in an isolated spot in the Snow Canyon campground, right under a golden locust tree, near big red rocks that harbor some type of nocturnal bird that calls out, "Janie, Janie," during the night.

It's snowing up north in bear country, and I hope they've all dug deep dens and are fast asleep by now, especially the little cubs with the blond undercoats. The reality of it all seems far away. Alaska—so far north, place of ice and aurora and polar bears.

I savor the warm canyon air around me, the full moon rising over tall walls, the sweet sound of the canyon wren, wishing Janie were here. Finally, I crawl into the tent with the dogs, all snuggled together in our warm sleeping bags, even though the night is balmy.

At first, I sleep well, a refuge from the reality of bad news. But soon come the dreams, like the stiff winds, and I toss and turn, wake and drift back off, but the dreams linger through the night, watching.

I dream of bears.

Giant chocolate brown Kodiak bears, *Ursus arctos middendorffi*, bearers of primal fear;

Black bears, *Ursus americanus*, typically shy yet responsible for more human deaths than any other bear;

The blue bear, *Ursus americanus emmonsii*, a subspecies of black bear found only in the glacier country of Southeast Alaska, their silver-blue coats blending in with blue glacial ice;

The Kermode or spirit bear, *Ursus americanus kermodei*, also a black bear, but with a creamy-white coat, found only in British Columbia;

Arctic polar bears, *Ursus maritimus*, coats so thick, holding the heat so well, so protective, that the bears can't be seen with thermal cameras;

And the golden brown bear, the grizzly, *Ursus arctos horribilis*, the bear with the hump on its back and dished nose, stunning in its terror.

The desert nights provide refuge, for there are no bears here, though the golden *Horribilis* now haunts my dreams.

First called "grisley" by Lewis and Clark, the name referred to the golden and gray tips of the animal's grizzled coat, the lighter-colored hairs that overlay the darker coat of the bear, but the bear was eventually classified formally by naturalist George Ord as *Ursus horribilis*. Ord made it clear he was not referring to its coat, but rather to its character. Ord lived in Philadelphia and based his classification on a stuffed specimen. Did he ever see a live grizzly? Did he know anyone who had?

I wake, sweating, not sure where I am at first, then see a hint of dawn reflected on the cliffs above, and I know the long claws, the huge yellow teeth are just a dream, one of many to come.

Here in the desert, I'm safe, for no bears come here where there's little food or water—except for *Horribilis*, who now visits every night since I found out Janie died.

Davie tells me later that they found tufts of the bear's golden hair caught in Janie's jacket buttons, but they never found the bear.

But I know where *Horribilis* is, he now follows me in my dreams, and I soon come to realize that I dare not leave the safety of the wide-open treeless badlands of the Utah desert.

Now I'm up, making coffee in the little pan on my one-burner propane stove, wary, watching as nearby shrubs are gradually lit by rising sun, losing their questionable shadow-shapes.

There are two kinds of sunrises in the desert. One is gradual and colorful, the sunrise with clouds that sun catches on its way through layers of horizon, giving fair warning. The other—no warning, as the sky is clear and the clouds aren't there to tell you how soon the sun will rise. There's a bit of golden light over the horizon, then sudden-ly, the sun's upon you. Just like *Horribilis*, no warning.

Leaning against my old truck, I savor the hot coffee, dreams fading like shadows.

All will be well, it will be another good long day in the desert, night far away. I pick up my sleeping bag and pad and toss them into the back of the truck.

Last night, after hearing about Janie, I found sleeping in a tent too claustrophobic—I could hear the ripping of nylon by sharp claws. I crawled out and slept on the ground, no false shelter to make me think I'm safe.

Today, I'll buy a can of bear spray to keep nearby, even here where there are no bears. *Ursus arctos horribilis* may disturb my dreams, but he'd better not try to disturb my sleep.

Sun's rays break over cliffs of red Navajo Sandstone streaked and layered with white. No one knows why the streaks—they're not actual layers. It gives the place a unique beauty, a mystery.

I have another cup of coffee, then a handful of candy corn. It leaves a sweet burning aftertaste in my mouth— pure sugar, the kind mammals crave, instant energy. Too much will kill you, though slowly.

Last night, after the bears left my dreams, I dreamed I was held by a man who loved me, and I cried.

He had no face.

A PARADOXICAL PAIR

It's nearly spring, and now I stop on my way back north, right smack in the heart of black bear country. It also happens to be the heart of Utah's Tusher Mountains, and the black-on-orange sign nearby reminds me that bears are a part of this landscape:

Warning! This is bear habitat. Store your food properly in the bear boxes. There is no guarantee of your safety while hiking and camping in bear country.

Below that is yet another sign, black-on-yellow:

Warning! Mountain lion frequenting area. Be alert. Solo hiking not recommended. Supervise children closely.

It's March fifth, and I walk through the tight canyon, my feet crunching in the ten inches of what was new snow a few days ago but which has now melted and refrozen, forming a thick crust.

The canyon is lined with castles and hoodoos of yellow tuft striped with white layers of ash that fell a million years ago from nearby volcanoes. The evening shadows feel menacing as they slowly grasp the light, dissipating it into small white points far away, far above—stars.

The small stream flows through the canyon when it's warm enough for water to move. Now, all is frozen, and night is falling with a chill. I set up my new tent—one with an open mesh top that I can see through, reducing my claustrophobia, with a rainfly for bad weather.

Next to me is one of the largest juniper trees I've ever seen, right on the bank of the seasonal stream. In the desert, such trees are rare and speak of great age, but here, where nurturing water is plentiful, they speak more of happiness and an easier life.

The tree sleeps the deep sleep of winter. It occurs to me I might not survive the night for the cold.

I've packed in, leaving my truck in the campground a mile or more below, which, though empty, sets too close to the freeway's noise. Besides, I want to experience true solitude, even though the dogs are along, now curled up in their down sleeping bags inside the tent.

And what of the signs warning of bears and lions? I can't account for the lions, but the bears should still be sleeping, deep in their hand–dug dens. Of what do they dream?

But it is possible that a bear or two has awakened early, hungry. What if such a bear smells my food and comes looking? Bears have a sense of smell much better than a bloodhound.

I once saw a black bear coming up the steep bank from the river below where I was living in Colorado, and I knew it would walk right below the tall deck I stood on, presumably unaware of my presence. This was before I knew they were such denizens of the world of scents.

Guests had cooked hamburgers on the deck's grill the previous evening, then had thoroughly cleaned it, aware we were in bear country.

Now nearby, the bear stood on its hind legs and turned its snout upwards, smelling the air, then promptly tried to climb the deck's posts. I said, "Hey, bear," and it retreated, though reluctantly.

Not long after, a bear, maybe the same one, climbed through a neighbor's open window, helping itself to the contents of their refrigerator, leaving tooth holes in their big jar of mayonnaise.

Now, in this cold and narrow canyon, I think of Janie, and I know I should tie my pack to a rope and hoist it into a tree, as it contains our breakfast of dog kibble and granola bars. But I somewhat foolishly decide to bank on the bears all being asleep, as I'm too cold to want to do anything but put out my sleeping bag and crawl inside, which I do, even though the evening sky is still partially blue through the mesh top of my tent.

It's soon blue–black, then pitch black, and I lie very still as the most amazing sight opens above me—a vault so full of stars you begin to fear they'll have to fall out of the sky, as it can't possibly hold them all.

And then they do begin to fall, and several blue–green meteors streak from horizon to horizon, silent, leaving trails of phosphorescence behind.

Bears are forgotten as I look up, my wool hat making my neck itch, the dark silent hoodoos looming over me. I pull off the hat and slide down into my sleeping bag, and when I awake, it's dawn and the hoodoos are turning gold in the first sunrays.

I slip from my bag, hair stiff with frost, and quickly make a cup of tea on my little propane stove. I'm so cold I can feel the warm drink as it makes its way down my throat to warm my chest.

Dogs happily gobble their kibble as I quickly take down the tent. We're soon on our way back down the small canyon, crunching through crusted snow, the movement warming us all.

I haven't walked more than 50 feet when I see it—fresh mountain lion tracks in the snow.

As the sun breaks over canyon rim, we finally exit the tight canyon and enter a clearing. I can see my truck parked below.

Afraid to look back, we trudge on down, jumping the little frozen creek. I feel a deep sense of relief as I unlock the door and we all pile in.

I later wonder at my paradoxical combination of fearlessness and cowardice.

WHATEVER MAKES YOU FEEL ALIVE

We're now further north, in the uplands near Price, Utah, and I can see Bruin Point high in the distance. I'm in a place I call Washtub Camp, as I found an old washtub full of bullet holes here, half buried in the sand.

It's evening, that time when the upwelling is the worst. Day is fine, then suddenly, from nowhere, something grabs inside you, clutches at your even keel, breaks any semblance of contentment, and makes you want to flee—run away, go anywhere, just go, flee, get out.

I wonder if it's not something deep in our DNA that tells us night is coming. Find your tribe for safety or be exposed to the many night predators that can take your life. Creatures like *Horribilis*.

Once night falls, the feeling ends, though it's sometimes replaced by an existential loneliness.

Night passed, it's now six a.m., and I suddenly feel Cassie stiffen next to me in my sleeping bag, half covered. I instinctively grab her collar, just as she starts growling.

There's something in camp.

I lie still, but Cassie tries to get away. I hold on tight as she begins to bristle, then I slip from my bag and half drag and half carry her to the nearby truck, where Weezee and Moki sleep. They, too, are on full alert. Once inside, I lock the doors. It's too dark to see anything.

Now the desert no longer feels safe, and I sleep in the truck from then on.

The dawn is out there, many miles away, slowly stalking the curvature of the earth, the sky turning a very subtle shade of color barely lighter than the horizon itself. The stars are still bright, but change is coming, and I feel a sense of relief, as light will also bring safety.

I see a glow far away, lights pushing the darkness away for awhile. Probably the tiny town of Columbia, nestled in the Books, or more likely, the Lila Canyon coal mine.

The villages of Sunnyside and East Carbon are lit up, and the glow of the bigger town of Price speaks of cozy houses with people sleeping in cozy beds.

From the rise I'm on, I can see the highway in the far distance, an occasional car traveling somewhere. But something now blocks the view and the car lights disappear. I turn on the truck lights, but it's gone.

Dawn slowly comes, sky gradually lighting.

I sit in the cab with the dogs and wait, afraid to get out to make a cup of coffee. It seems like it takes hours, but by seven it's light enough to see the rolling grasslands, and I soon step out of the truck and fire up my one–burner stove for coffee.

I look for mountain lion tracks, like I saw back in the Tushers, but instead find antelope tracks in the dirt all around camp. This long gradual upland I'm camped on is a perfect home for them. Antelope are very curious, but my sense of safety is gone nonetheless.

The beloved sun now shoots great rays over the ramparts of the Books, telling the world it's arrived. A new day begins—will I ever be free of my fears? Will I ever find a home? Will I ever know exactly what happened to Janie, and do I want know?

A thin strip of light along the horizon tells me a thick cover of clouds has come in during the night. I get out my little weather radio and turn the crank to charge it up.

You're listening to NOAA weather radio. Tomorrow will be windy and partly cloudy, with lows in the 50s. A southwest flow will develop into a trough through the week, and hazardous weather is predicted Tuesday through Wednesday, with heavy snowfall above 8,000 feet. Unusually warm temperatures will return for the rest of the week. Flash flooding is predicted for Arches National Park.

As the sky lightens, the distant mountains take on more depth, changing from cardboard cutouts to mountains with shadow mountains behind. I can now see the faint outline of the little two-track road that brought me here through these grassy uplands. The edges of the morning sky turn into fiery strips of gold where the thick clouds let the light shine through.

Deep blues light up the western sky above the distant Wasatch Plateau to the west. Back to the east, I can make out the lights of someone up early, their car winding up the rugged cliffs of the Books on the windy exposed Horse Canyon Road.

Now, finally, the contours and lay of the land are revealed, the grasslands a dull yellow. A purple shaft lights up the clouds directly where the sun will soon rise, and maroons and reds streak across the sky like a carpet spread out for royalty.

Now Cassie's ears are perked, and I follow her gaze— there, in the distance, two dark figures run across the hill— antelope! Are they running from a lion? Or are they running with the sheer exuberance that sunrise brings?

The eastern sky glows with layer upon layer of color, and I think back to the evening before and the desolation I felt. This sunrise is the consolation, the opposite of all the loneliness of the previous night.

The Books are now a somber blue, backlit by rising sun, a long flow of jagged cliffs that end just past the single point of Mount Elliot on down where they turn at Green River and go east into Colorado. Mount Elliot looks more like an upside-down V than a mountain.

A black dot with wings flies towards the west, an early-rising raven on its way to something important—maybe a drink of water.

The day begins in earnest, and it's time to take the dogs for a walk, even though it's chilly. I can see for miles—no bears here unless way up in the forested high flanks of the Tavaputs Plateau high above the rampart of the Books.

I make out a few lone splashes of yellow in the high distance on their slopes, aspens from last fall who refused to let the winds take their golden dowry. Winds will return soon, according to the weather radio, howling through the high ramparts like the fierce wolves who once wandered this country. Perhaps next time I'm here I'll find a leaf that's floated all the way down from way up there.

The antelope have stopped, now grazing in the distance, probably on the gray shadscale or winterfat draped with seeds so white they look like snow.

From nowhere, or maybe from the wintry clouds above, a memory comes. It was late at night—Janie liked to drive late at night, hell, all through the night, especially if the moon was full. She said it gave her a sense of freedom.

We were going to see her friends at the Riviera Restaurant in Glenwood Springs, Colorado, where she once worked. The bar would close at two a.m., and it was one a.m., and we were still more than an hour away. We finally made it, but only after Janie pushed her old VW Bug to the limits, rattling down the highway way too fast while I held on.

At one point, I protested, and she said, "Chin, hon, you're not really alive unless you're having an adventure."

"What exactly do you call an adventure?" I asked.

Janie replied, "Anything that makes you feel alive."

"That's tautological," I replied.

"Chin, you need to hurry up and get out of college. It's filling up your brain with big words, and pretty soon there won't be any room for anything else. But no, it's not circular, if that's what you're trying to say. Adventure is life, or it should be. If it's not, you're not really living."

"What about all those people who have to work every day? Are they all dead then?"

"Yup. Zombies, or at least until they have an adventure."

The clouds now turn a deep blue-gray. Sun will finally break through after several hours, when it finally traverses above the clouds, but until then, it's a gray morning, all promise of adventure now gone.

I can see that blue highway stretching all the way to Green River, straight as an arrow to where it drops off Horse Bench and onto the floor of the ancient Mancos Shale, the ancient Cretaceous bed of the Western Interior Seaway.

Sun finally breaks through and each yellow stalk of squirreltail grass turns gold until the entire upland is shining like a vast treasure. Why search for buried gold when it's right here for the taking?

I break off one of the brittle stems, now long dried in desert sun since last spring's growth, and stick it in the brim of my hat. This evening, I'll take it out and let it remind me of this morning's optimism. Maybe it will help ease the angst.

WE CAN TALK ABOUT IT WHEN WE ALL GET TO HEAVEN

Time to move on, pretend I have somewhere to go, something to do, but you have to stop eventually, stop somewhere, and I have no destination. Actually, I do, but it's still too early to go to Alaska. I'm treading water.

Evening comes, and I'm once again on Horse Bench. Even though the sky above has cleared, dark clouds are beginning to circle the horizon, coming in from the south. They're stretched out, elongated, with bumps and humps on their backs, looking like a flotilla of ancient mosasaurs coming to scout out the territory, alligator-like with their long snouts and tails.

Maybe they're looking for the ancient sea that once covered this land and where they swam freely. The only water around now is what they'll bring with them.

Or maybe they're scouting out the territory for the bigger clouds that are predicted to bring rains by midnight. I'm camped in a spot that will turn to mud, so I hope the main flotilla will wait until morning so I can retreat, unscathed.

I'm now coughing from the incoming humidity, and my throat's a bit sore. From nowhere, a song comes from the past, my childhood, and I hum along.

Come home, come home it's suppertime,
The shadows lengthen fast.
Come home, come home it's suppertime.
I'm going home at last.

My dad always sang this song in church, and the tune comes back strong and true to memory, though not many of the words. Of course, it's about death and feeds on poignancy and the false hope that after we die we get to go to our true homes and a better place. It's a dangerous sentiment, thinking something better is waiting after death. I'd rather find my home while I'm still alive.

Janie found her home—it was on the white sand beaches of Hawaii. She only returned to her childhood home in Alaska and its people when they were dying, and she never stayed long.

She always went back to Hawaii because she had too many memories in Alaska, good and bad, but too many, all cluttering up her brain and preventing new and better memories from being made—or at least that's what she told me.

Did Janie not really want to go when she left Hawaii, somehow knowing it would lead to her death? I don't really want to go north, but something's pushing me along—will it lead to my own death?

Alaska has even higher mountains than my childhood home of Colorado, and I've had enough of high mountains, snow, cold, and those high fortresses of such beauty that you forget how easy it is to die up there. And the thick forests call to you, forests where you can't see out and you can't see in, where you can get lost and not even know it until it's beyond repair. I almost did that a couple of times.

And forests are good bear habitat.

My home is the big empty desert, but sometimes I feel the mountains haunting me, calling to me. It's a siren song, the same one that lured Janie back.

My cell phone rings, and I can tell from the caller ID that it's Davie, checking up on me.

"Everything OK?" he asks.

"Fine," I reply, glad to hear his voice. "You?"

"Fine. I'm getting ready to head out into the Triangle."

"The Dolores Triangle?" I ask.

"Well, not the Bermuda one, for sure."

"There's the Alaska Triangle," I pause, thinking of Janie.

Davie ignores me. "I was talking to a rancher from Glade Park, and he says the roads are clear out there. There's a storm coming in, but it doesn't look like it will do much here. I'm gonna go in after it dries out, maybe in a few days."

"Are you still looking for the contact?" I ask, referring to where two formations meet, in this case, the Burro Canyon and Cedar Mountain, which he's been studying.

"Yeah, I've been looking at the maps, and I'm pretty sure I can find it."

He pauses, then adds, "Say, Chin?"

I hate it when he says that, and I know what's coming.

"Yeah?"

"There's a nice little house down the street from me here in Junction. I called the guy, and you can have dogs. It's cheap. Nothing fancy, but looks nice enough. Has a big fenced yard."

"Thanks for thinking of me, but you know I can't afford to rent right now. I'm almost broke."

"You could get a job here at the dino museum—they're looking for someone to help at the quarry. You'd love it. You have the qualifications. I can help you with a rental deposit and all that."

"I appreciate it, Davie, but I want to head up north."

"I wondered if you were still thinking that way. You know, there's nothing really more to know about all that. I talked to Roddie, and he says they never found the bear. It was just a case of Janie being in the wrong place at the wrong time. She probably startled the bear, and they think maybe it had cubs. Why not just stay here for the summer?"

"It sounds really good, Davie, but you know me."

"Look, you could stick it out for once. If you got claus-trophobic, you could sleep on the back porch or even go camping for a few days. You know the gypsy blood eventu-ally starts to run thin."

"You know it's more than that."

"You need a home, Chin. Everyone needs a home. Even me. Once I get this fieldwork done, I may quit this job. The Utah State Geological Survey says they want to hire me, maybe in Price. I want to buy a little house and have a gar-den. I guess we can talk about it later."

"We can talk about it when we all get to Heaven," I joke, thinking of Janie, who always ended conversations she didn't like that way. The fact that Janie wasn't religious always added to the irony.

Davie sighs, then is gone.

ORION'S GONE A'HUNTING

I wake in the shadow of the high jagged ridge above me, backlit by dawn like a cardboard cutout. A few scattered wisps of clouds catch the sun's early rays, tinted a light salmon color.

A dark shadow moves in the distance, and for a moment I imagine I'm on the wide savannas of Africa, an elephant galloping through the yellow grasses. Then I see it's a truck on the highway a mile or so away.

The clouds have now turned pink, and I think I should take a photo of the sunrise, but it's too cold. The water jug had a thin layer of ice on it earlier when I made coffee.

The dogs are restless, wanting out, then jumping back in after their breakfast, curling up to stay warm and sleep.

It's almost eight a.m., and only just now can one make out the landscape enough to not really need a flashlight. The sun still hasn't cleared the ramparts of the Books, and several spires stand backlit by the palest of blue skies, dotted with pink clouds.

I was up by six-thirty, having gone to sleep at nine the previous night. In spite of getting up once to pee, I feel rested. The dogs all ran out in the dark when I got up, which worries me because of coyotes and lions.

A black bear was killed a day or so ago over by the little town of Elmo. It wouldn't go down when tranquilized, so they killed it. The paper showed a photo of it being harassed by Utah Department of Wildlife hounds. It must've come down from the Wasatch plateau, looking for food.

Now the day begins in earnest as the sun finally crests the Books, lighting everything with a harsh light and chasing away the ice on my water jug. Clouds turn white and sky turns blue. Last night's angst is gone. It's another day on a spinning planet on the edge of the Milky Way Galaxy.

Last night Amtrak came by, and I could see the cars in the distance, all lit up. It seemed incongruous to see all those people passing through the Big Empty, playing cards, eating, listening to music, talking, unaware of a solo camper in the blackness just out their windows.

I can see a thick seam of what looks to be coal, high in the Books where it could never be mined, a black continuous layer that streaks through the high cliffs like a ribbon. I at first thought it was the shadow of an overhang, but binoculars showed otherwise.

I try to plan the day, but it's a hopeless endeavor that seems to involve a bit of hubris, as if I could know what was coming.

I know there's a storm coming in with lots of wind, and once again, I feel alone, restless, and hopeless. Just one storm after another, such is life. The pain of Janie's death cuts through me like a hot knife through soft butter.

A desolation sets in, one with no cure, except maybe going to sleep. Like the bears, I sometimes wish I could sleep through the long winter, hibernate.

The darkness seeps into everything, even my soul, and I want to forget it all now, be someone else, my memories like strange night creatures who fly north each winter, happy in the ache of the cold.

I suddenly feel tired and listless, and the thought of breaking camp and going somewhere else seems too difficult, so we just hang around camp all day. I dread the night for fear of bears—night bears far more dangerous then the wildest grizzly, bears that would devour your most precious and necessary of things—your sanity.

I want to surround myself with light, music, laughter, colorful paintings of gold and red autumn aspen leaves–but instead, I sit alone in the empty desert until evening comes, then the darkness.

I tuck the dogs into their beds in the pickup, then sit in my camp chair in the dark and cold, alone in the silence of the brightest of stars, alone with the night bears, for it's the only way to subdue them.

You must fight them one on one, one at a time, under the winter night sky, alone, for all other victories are merely illusions. Alone. One on one.

And now I'm tired. Just thinking about the pain, letting it shear through me, tires me out and makes me want to sleep, but I know sleeping is very risky. Night bears hide over the horizon, their ears sometimes poking up like tiny rocks on distant mountains, but once I sleep, they'll be here in a flash.

So, I pull my sleeping bag up to my ears and pretend to take a short nap. If the bears think I'm just napping and will easily awake, maybe they'll leave me alone.

Orion stands bold in the night sky above me, destined to forever hold his stiff stance, watching as my species fizzles out, gradually eaten by bears.

MOKI'S GONE

I awake and immediately know something's wrong. I let the dogs out, but Moki stays in the truck, motionless.

I then know she's passed.

I lift her body from the truck, still on her dog bed, and lay her gently on the ground.

How can this be? How could she leave so quietly, without telling us?

Sitting by her in shock, I note the look of release on her spotted face. She'd been failing, I knew that, and I'd taken her to the vet, but they could find nothing wrong.

She'd been off and on with eating, something unlike Moki, who loved food, having come from a shelter that underfed the dogs to save money.

Finally, I make a cup of coffee and sit in my camp chair next to her silent body as Weezee sniffs her, though Cassie seems to show no interest. Finally, I pull a small blanket over her, giving her privacy—or perhaps keeping myself from looking at her, from acknowledging her death.

Moki's gone.

It happened so quickly. Just the previous day she'd been lazing around camp, though I had noted she didn't want to eat. And at one point she went missing, and I walked around calling her, looking, until she finally emerged from a small nearby wash. She always stayed with us, so this was another clue, and I'd been puzzled by it.

I sit, quietly mourning, then get up and lift her back into the truck. I drive slowly to the vet in Price, who unloads her body as I pay for the cremation. They'll call when her ashes are returned, and that's all there is to it. I walk back out the door, Moki gone forever.

Back out at camp, it hits me hard, her absence, the lack of her furry face in my rear-view mirror, where she always rode, maybe so she could likewise see my face, as she had a touch of separation anxiety. She'd spent her first year at a shelter in California's Gold Country where they'd tried everything possible to cure a skin rash she had.

The shelter had finally given up and decided to put her to sleep, but Moki had a champion, a staff person who demanded she get one more chance with a new vet. This vet was able to cure her, and my friend, a volunteer there, called me to see if I wanted her.

"Moki needs a good home," Diana said over the phone. "She's developed every bad trick in the book and needs someone who's patient."

I was there two days later, adopting the beautiful Australian Shepherd-Blue Heeler mix, and when I went to take her home, she rolled onto her back on the shelter floor and wouldn't get up. It took two volunteers to lift her into the back of my truck, where she promptly peed.

But back in Utah, Moki soon became one of the pack, running free in the desert. She always had a smile on her goofy face, perhaps to trick you into thinking she wasn't as smart as she really was, which was dog-gone smart.

"She wouldn't have had a chance without you," Diana tries to console me when I call to tell her Moki's passed. "She was adopted once before you got her, and they returned her the next day. She was lucky she had you. You gave her a good life."

I want to return to one of Moki's favorite camp spots, where she would bark at the hot-air balloon that passed overhead each morning.

But I make it only to Washtub Camp, where the angst and futility hit hard.

What exactly is it that we mourn in the face of such loss? The life that's gone, yes, but there's more. Perhaps it's the passage of shared time that's gone, a segment of life ended, never to be recovered. The finality of it is stunning.

"Life is short," people say, and we nod our heads in agreement, but it really doesn't hit you until you're the one caught by that brevity. Then it hits you hard, like the front edge of an incoming storm, one that will set a record this time for sure. It hits with a coldness, a harshness, a blunt force that makes you struggle to catch your breath.

And we grieve until time eases it somewhat. We look for that face, that presence we can't accept is no longer there—surely she's just asleep in the other room. How can it be that she's gone? So sudden, so final.

And Cassie and Weezee now become the only constants I have as life swirls all around—they're like rocks in a roiling stream.

No stability, no continuity, except them. They're always there with me no matter where I go—Snow Canyon, Washtub Camp, Alien Camp—time flows around us, changes things day by day, and they're the only constant in the flux—until they're gone, then I realize stability is just an illusion. They're also flowing along with the rest of the stream and will soon disappear around the bend along with it all.

And so, Moki's gone. I think of the little toy dinosaur I teased her with, and I feel bad, like somehow I could have done better for her. She was such a sweet spirit—there's something about those Australian Shepherds.

And the little black raccoon that I saw last night, the one with the white mask, when it's gone, nobody will even notice. As if somehow having a human miss you makes your life more worthwhile.

And so, we'll continue on, me and Cassie and Weezee, until the next bend and another of us is gone, just like Moki. Remembered only by the others, and when they're gone, even that memory will be gone.

Based on estimates of the total number of people ever born and their longevity, the Population Reference Bureau estimates that 108 billion humans have lived on earth. We have no idea how many dogs and cats and other forms of life have inhabited our planet.

All I know is there have been many mournings.

The river flows deep and strong and no one can turn its tide when the time comes. Maybe it's best to just accept it for what it is.

Why does pain make me claustrophobic, wanting to flee to the wilds? The ache becomes almost too much, followed by the longing to return to where we were happy with Moki—but instead of returning, we go another direction.

INTO THE TRIANGLE

Davie calls yet again, leaving a message that he would still like for me to join him in the Dolores Triangle, helping him with his geology research.

He's trying to divert me from going north, I suspect, even though he says he would like some company way out there, on top of the huge mesas filled with dino bones.

I've camped near these endless graveyards before, places that hold the remnants of species that once flourished and maybe even had emotions like ours, species long gone and bones now fossilized, species we have never heard of nor ever will. Did they mourn one another?

I suspect that he's wanting me along to help avoid that same old angst that comes from staring too long, too alone, at the maw of the universe, too far from the illusionary comforts of civilization. Too many stars in the night sky.

Alone out there with deep geologic time right smack in front of you, unlike many regions where vegetation hides all. This is why geologists journey to the American West— to study the Earth in its naked beauty.

I hesitate to commit to going, as I'm on the edge myself, missing Moki and trying to comprehend the incomprehensible. But finally, I call him back and say yes, I'll come out.

Maybe we can help each other work through some of the grief.

"It's not too hard to find," he assures me, "Just follow BLM 107. There's only a couple of signs."

Once out there, I find the only signs are on large rocks bearing somewhat cryptic white painted letters worn by time to near illegibility, such as "D LR S R VER" (Dolores River).

For years I've seen the long upland of the Dolores Triangle, technically the end of Colorado's Uncompahgre Plateau, an island cut off from the rest of that ancient uplift by a deep canyon called Unaweep. The Triangle is called that because it's bounded by the Colorado and Dolores rivers on two sides and the Colorado-Utah border on the third.

It's a somewhat arbitrary designation, though its inaccessibility is less arbitrary, as its river sides are bounded by high cliffs, and the Utah-Colorado side climbs into the highlands of Pinion Mesa, which harbor aspen, mule deer, elk, and black bears.

To enter the Triangle from the west, one must ford the Dolores River, which is crossable only when the river flows less than 160 cfs, typically in the fall. The Colorado River is too deep to ford. The eastern access to the Triangle climbs step narrow switchbacks with miles over dirt roads that become impassible when wet.

It's one of those landscapes that many see because of its visibility from the interstate far below, though few visit. I've seen this upland for many years while traversing the lower Mancos shales of the Big Empty, and because of the slant of the huge mesa, one can see the long serpentine curves of its many intriguing redrock canyons, places lost in distance and mystery.

If you stop your car and pull out the binoculars, you can even see an occasional Entrada arch or two, and as the landscape rises from the river cliffs, one can easily make out the 1.8 billion-year-old black basement rock of the Black Canyon Complex with huge red Wingate cliffs riding atop its dark waves, and on top of it all the beautiful pink curves of sinuous Entrada Sandstone.

I'm in Colorado by mid-afternoon, wishing I'd gotten an earlier start. There's something about new routes into rugged unknown backcountry that breeds a sense of trepidation when alone.

I climb the twisty hairpin curves of Colorado National Monument and am soon into the high uplands and straight roads of Glade Park. I drive and drive the miles, thinking I'll never get there before dark, wherever "there" is, and soon I can see Utah's La Sal Mountains to the southwest, a small cluster of points on the horizon.

Soon, I'm looking out into country that I know well— the distant Bookcliffs bounding the long white expanses of Mancos shale, the long anticlines of Dome Plateau, the yellowish lower country of Yellow Cat Flats with its Morrison hills, and the tall spire of Castle Rock, all bounding the Big Empty. Tiny moving dots on the flats mark the freeway lanes.

The road has gone from paved to gravel to sand as I parallel the redrock Wingate cliffs, crossing places where the normally dry washes have recently run, leaving wet pools in the road. I'm soon by a large corral that marks the end of the sandy road and the beginning of the impassible-when-wet smectites of the Brushy Basin Morrison.

The road narrows and gets rougher, and I soon cross the deep and tricky Coates Creek, then climb a long rutted shelf road with a big dropoff. I'm now in blackbrush country and can see forever. After climbing yet another shelf road, I'm on top of a huge mesa rimmed with sheer yellow cliffs, the Cedar Mountain Formation, rich with dino bone.

My apprehension fades upon seeing Davie's pickup camper.

We make three different camps in five days as Davie measures a huge cliff section, and I help him mark paleo-currents which show which direction the layers were laid down. And each night, we sit in our camp chairs and talk, the cold eventually prompting me to pull out my propane heater to keep us warm.

Finally, when we're tired and talked out, he climbs into his camper and I lean against my truck, Cassie and Weezee snug asleep inside. And I wonder where Moki and Janie are, feel their loss, feel the distance and immensity and futility of life in an unfathomable universe.

Soon the moon begins to rise, taking me by welcome surprise as I've lost track of what day it is, its light shimmering on the Colorado River far below. Tiny headlights light up the freeway crossing the Big Empty, and I wonder where everyone's going, thinking back to a time not long ago when it was rare to see another car on its long desert stretches.

Early one morning, Davie still asleep, I let the dogs out and immediately hear a loud and deep growling. The dogs hesitate, stay by the truck, then bark, ears perked up.

Was it a nearby lion? The Triangle supposedly has a lot of mountain lions, though I would suspect they'd be higher up, more in the timbered uplands where the deer live. After awhile, the dogs relax. Whatever it was, it's gone.

After a week of helping Davie, he's finished and wanting to go home, get a hot meal, and take a hot shower. I decide to stay, as I'm finding the isolation of the Triangle healing in its own way.

Davie leaves me the rest of his food and water, then slowly drives off. I feel a twinge of aloneness, followed by a moment of euphoria. It's been a long time since I was in a place so truly remote.

The days on the Triangle are long and raw, on the edge of the planet, the edge of the weather, the edge of time, the edge of distance, the edge of eternity, and I feel every minute of it. It's a raw and wild place of distances difficult to describe, almost like being a raven and floating above everything with a feeling of opportunity, of hope, of so many places to go, to explore, to run away to, to hide in, to disappear into—a landscape of great open-heartedness, great open-mindedness, and great freedom.

Each day I explore, though I also spend hours gazing into the distance, thinking of how truly finite Moki's life was, a short nine years, how truly finite my own life will be, like a speck of dust blowing in a breeze—you catch a glimpse in the sunlight for a brief moment and it's gone. It's not a particularly desultory feeling, it's just how it is.

Being on that upland above everything, I can feel the atmosphere, and it feels like the planet is more sky than earth. I can look and see a topographic map laid out below me, deep canyons whose rims I've stood upon.

It's a landscape of memory—I can see all these places where I've walked, laughed, talked around campfires, slept, and places where I've shared place and time with friends both human and canine. It almost seems like a map of my past that I'm looking down upon.

Look! There's Grasshopper Camp, where a grasshopper climbed up my longjohn leg one dark night, and I jumped up and hopped around, thinking it was a scorpion.

And there's Carnotite Camp, where I found a big petrified log filled with yellow radioactive carnotite, over by Fin Canyon.

And there's the old abandoned Thompson Springs Gun Range, wooden targets old and weathered, next to an old stock pond thick with rabbitbrush and tamarisk. I remember how I hid the old rifle there that my dad left me, not wanting to carry it around in my truck, leaving instructions for Davie to find it on his way over from Colorado.

And there's Washtub Camp, where I camped with Moki the night before she died.

Up on the Triangle, the days of my life are mapped out below me, and everywhere I look there's a memory. So many that I have to ask, just how old am I, anyway?

But it's not that I'm so old, it's just that I've spent so much of my life out here wandering around. No wonder this whole desert seems so indelibly marked in my brain. My neural connections have desert sand in them.

So, I spend many days looking out at the distance, feeling the absence of Moki, the absence of many others who are gone, of Janie, and when evening comes I open a can of soup and sit by a little fire and think, tired and weary in a way that goes beyond the physical.

And each day it seems impossible that I'm in this mysterious place I've always wanted to visit. It seems like a dream. All the times I've looked from far away at the unexplored uplands and redrock canyons flowing from Pinion Mesa, and at a certain point I just have to go to bed.

I wake in the middle of the night and the moon's still high in the night sky, bright, clear, and I can hear coyotes. It's a paradox—a longing for this place, this place where one really doesn't belong and couldn't survive for long.

I shake my head, crawl deeper into my sleeping bag and go back to sleep, dreaming about a warm bed in a house somewhere far from the Dolores Triangle, some place safe and cozy and not so on the edge.

But when you go home, assuming you have one, at first you're happy to be there, especially when you see on the weather station that it's snowing in the Triangle. You feel a sense of elation that you survived and beat the bad weather, and you take a hot shower, then drink hot tea and luxuriate in being in a house—no rattlers or storms to worry about.

But after a couple of days it hits you like a wall cloud with high winds and lightning—something's missing. You feel empty and miss the distance, the loneliness, aloneness, and you want to be back out there.

Deep inside, you know you have to go back out soon, there's no choice. And so once again the cycle starts, and you get out the maps. After awhile your cozy secure shelter feels overwhelming and you want to be outside, so you sit on the back porch just to feel the breeze. After awhile, you want to go sleep in your truck, but you know the neighbors would wonder why.

So, that money you've been saving for emergencies—well, this qualifies as an emergency, and you go buy a new sleeping bag, even though your old bag works just fine. And it's not just any sleeping bag, but an expensive 880-fill down, specially treated for moisture and rated to infinity below zero, the absolute best for Alaska.

And you know it's a good investment, better than money in the bank, because once you get up there, you'll need it, especially if you decide to never come back.

HEIRLOOM HONEYSUCKLE

I get a call from the vet to come and get Moki's ashes. They're in a plastic bag inside a square stiff-cardboard box, heavier than I expected, and I feel strangely emotionless when the vet-tech hands them to me with a look of sympathy on her face.

"I'm so sorry," she offers, and I know it's part of her job, probably something she does all too often, hand people boxes with their friend's ashes and say she's sorry.

I'm staying at Davie's, as he's gone to Denver on business for a week. I'm watching his dogs, Jasper and Buddy, and they and my dogs laze around in his big back yard with its huge maple trees and lilac bushes.

Moki has spent plenty of time here, too, lounging around in the thick cool grass, waiting for someone to come by on the bike path so she can run over to the fence and bark, tail wagging, hoping for a friendly hand to poke through and pet her.

I've decided to take Moki's ashes to Washtub Camp, one of her favorite places in the desert. We've spent many days and nights there hiking, sleeping, and eating, which was one of Moki's favorite activities.

It's nice to be indoors, no worries if a storm comes through, but I soon find myself restless and unsettled, like something's wrong.

Finally, two mornings after I pick up the ashes, I wake before dawn, the kind of waking that's sudden and stark.

It's still dark, so I get up and go sit in the big leather recliner in the living room. Sitting there in the dark, it finally comes to me—Moki was a homebody, a comfort hound, as she'd had little comfort before I got her. She loved big grassy yards and thick indoor rugs, preferably close to or in the kitchen.

And though she loved camping and hiking with us in the desert, I always felt she'd been somewhat shorted by not living with someone who was a gourmet cook and would slip her goodies under the table at dinnertime.

I make a cup of coffee and sit back down, sipping it slowly. The more I think about it, taking her ashes back out to the desert doesn't seem right. I open the curtains and watch out the big window as the sun slowly climbs the top of the distant cliffs.

The box of ashes sits on the coffee table, and Moki's death again seems incomprehensible and unexpected. Not long ago, I had Moki, and now all I have is this small box.

Suddenly, I feel resolved. I slowly get up and take the box to the back yard, into a far corner where honeysuckle tangles itself into a mass of tiny pink flowers quietly announcing that spring is here.

And as the sun now tops over the mountains, I carefully spread Moki's ashes where they can nurture the bush and its tiny blossoms.

It seems like the right thing to do, and even though I know Moki's gone, I still feel this is where she would want to be, not in the wilds of the desert. To her, this would be home.

I go back inside and finish my coffee, a smooth Ethiopian Yirgacheffe sent by Diana out in California, then sit back down in the big leather chair, wondering how much longer I'll be able to go out to the wilds myself, how long before I, too, relish simply sitting and watching the world go by, wishing someone would slip me goodies.

Scientists say the earth's magnetic poles shift every so often and wobble around, and I'm suddenly aware that the poles of my own life are likewise shifting, an event seemingly out of the blue, just like Moki's passing.

And time is also quickly shifting—I need to head north, where the summers pass quickly, where they're even briefer than Moki's life, even briefer than Janie's.

STAR BEARS

Sometimes the back of my truck feels like a coffin, so I curl up and sleep in the cab, me and Cassie.

It's cramped but feels safe and cozy, and I can look up through the windows to see if the stars are out or if some flotilla of clouds has arrived.

Weezee doesn't seem to mind being in the back alone, as long as she has her big fluffy down sleeping bag, and she can always stick her nose through the cab window if she needs company. A few times she's even crawled through and slept with us, though she's safe and secure back there under the truck topper.

We're camped in the desert near Green River, and my weather radio says there's a 20 percent chance of rain after midnight. I roll down the window a bit to see if the air's more humid, which it is, and a breeze is picking up.

I imagine something slipping up next to me, and I quickly roll up the window. Cassie sleeps, no worries, so it must be my imagination.

I soon wake to the pitter patter of raindrops on the pickup roof—so much for that 20 percent chance. I had carefully put everything inside before I went to bed—my camp chair, my stove, my cooler—knowing I might have to leave during the night. I had promised myself I'd go at the first hint of rain, as the road out is long and rough and pure bentonite clay.

But instead, I slip back asleep, thinking I'll be sure to wake if it truly rains.

What I didn't expect was sleet—that silent mix of rain and snow that quietly soaks everything. What wakes me isn't the sleet, but the sudden cold. I turn on the truck lights and am overwhelmed to see a full–on blizzard, several inches of snow already on the ground.

I wasn't prepared for this, nor apparently was the weatherman. I slip on my boots, then turn the key and start the truck.

Who knows what will happen if I stay? I'm not prepared to hole up in a major storm. I slide my way down the narrow two–track, the wet snow quickly icing my wipers. I stop for a bit, windshield covered with snow, until the heater's warm enough to de–ice everything.

I carry on, wondering what I'll do if I slide off the road. I'm no more than a mile away from my camp when snow turns to rain, and by the time I reach the main road, all is dry. I'm thankful as I drive into the night, now finally heading north.

Driving along half asleep, I feel like I'm under the control of someone or something else. After driving an hour through the black night, I see the Milky Way girding the night sky, and I know I've driven through the storm.

I stop at a pullover and make a quick cup of coffee, then get back on the road, cranking up the heat, still cold in spite of Cassie snuggled up against me. It's four a.m. and won't be dawn until seven. A good time to travel, no traffic, if I can stay awake, and if not, I'll pull over and sleep for a few hours.

I think about what's now become a compulsion to go north. It's a good time to go, and maybe I'll be lucky and have good weather, unless I hit spring storms. The tourists won't be on the road this early in the season and maybe I can find lots of campsites. Besides, I miss Moki, and maybe it will help take my mind off her death.

I pull over to let the dogs out for a minute. We're now on top of Soldier Summit, on the edge of lonely and empty, and as the dogs sniff around, I look up at the night sky. Salt Lake City is about an hour or so away, and the night sky is clear and chilly.

There, hanging in the north, are the seven stars of Ursa Major, the Great Bear. One of its stars points to Polaris, the North Star, which is also the tip of Ursa Minor, the Little Bear.

Here, in the U.S., as well as in Canada, these constellations are known as the Big and Little Dippers, though other countries call them the Starry Plough, the Wagon, and the Ladle. The Big Dipper is featured on the Alaska state flag.

The image of these two constellations as bears lingers in the mythology of many different peoples, including the Iroquois, Algonquians, and the Lakota, among others.

Looking into the dark forest, I suddenly again feel fear, as if something is nearby, and I call the dogs, getting them into the truck. But before I get in, I once again take in the night sky for a brief moment, hand on the door handle as I look up.

Hanging above me the Milky Way shimmers, star-studded like a massive pathway through the sky for the giant star-bears. It feels very distant, yet very close, maybe too close, and I suddenly feel panicked and jump into the truck, locking the door.

I'm puzzled, wondering why I'm now so afraid, after spending years camping alone, for the most part fearless. And I realize that now, death seems so close, as if following me, stalking me, just around the corner, behind me, watching, inevitable, relentless.

And I know, now that it's spring, the further north I go, the more bears that will be waking—great bears, major bears, little bears, minor bears, and the bear that killed Janie.

I want to go home, to that place that now feels as mythical as the bears above me, as unattainable.

An intense longing fills me, a hopeless tangle of comfort and freedom and security and wildness and stability and serendipity, a feeling of wanting to fly with abandon while standing safely on the ground at the same time.

How much of this longing is predisposed by evolution, a genetic need for the safety of a human tribe around us? And how much is predisposed by a gene that two percent of us have, the wanderer's gene, a gene that evolved to ensure we humans, we wanderers, continue to enlarge our territory for survival?

I feel caught in the middle with no hope of resolution, always doomed, no matter which way I go.

Shivering, I crank up the heater, leaning back into the comfort and security of my truck, then pull back onto the highway.

I'll drive on through the night, through the vast folds of the Milky Way, going north, north to a landscape filled with bears—polar bears, black bears, brown bears, blue glacier bears, and even spirit bears the color of frothy cappuccino.

PART IV

NORTHERN DREAMS

Yukon Territory / Alaska

A BEAR STORY

And so begins another story, one set in the far north above the 49th parallel, that boundary defined between the U.S. and Canada by the Anglo-American Treaty.

In 1818, the U.S. and Great Britain decided that the straight-line boundary of the 49th parallel would be easier to survey than the pre-existing boundaries—boundaries based on waterways that changed with each new snowmelt, braiding and meandering like the stories of our lives. And thus became the great boundary that marks the stories of Canada and the U.S.

Like water, which is vital to life, stories help us define who we are. Like the banks of a river, our stories give us a frame of reference for the streams of our lives, and whether the stories are true or not is of minor importance.

And most critically, our stories give us a place to call home, a place where we can create our own roots and past. Each time we recall a story, it changes a little, ever so subtly, into the recollection itself, until finally the actual event is far removed from the telling.

We tend to think that the past is fixed and gone, yet we can change it by how we remember it. Recalling memories in different ways can help us re-interpret the past and create new future paths. Stories let us look back at our past with a deeper understanding.

This provides us a form of solace, of comfort, for we can thereby rewrite our lives, our own histories, to whatever suits us, making our real past our true past, a past more suited to our own visions of what we wanted our lives to be, which they then become.

And this is how we heal ourselves.

And so, this is a story of how I was healed—with the help of the story of a bear.

BEAR DREAMS

And now, I've finally arrived in the north, in Whitehorse, Yukon Territory, to begin rewriting the part of my story that includes Janie. I can't change the fact that she's dead, but perhaps a better understanding of it will help me make it into a story I can more easily comprehend.

It's mid-May, and as I walk the riverfront park along the mighty Yukon River, all is draped in a mist that seems to swirl up from the past, bearing apparitions of old steamships, river ghosts, bedraggled prospectors, and tired mushers on worn dogsleds—as well as wolves, moose, and mosquitoes, which may not be apparitions at all.

A sign by the river reads:

Bears are waking up! Bears are active from April to November. Avoid animal encounters which can lead to bears dying needlessly.

I wonder about the humans who die needlessly from bears, and somehow I suspect it's a much smaller number, though the woman who was killed on a boardwalk at Laird Hot Springs back down the road certainly qualifies. She was on her way to Alaska to start a new life.

And now, here on the Yukon River, it's break-up, that time each spring when the thick brittle ice shatters against itself with groans and creaks and moans that make the apparitions in the swirling fog seem even more real.

Like the river, the town seems unsettled, as if it might itself just break up and float on out through Alaska to the Bering Sea. Whitehorse is the warmest part of the Yukon, and spring is a time of restlessness here for not just the ice, but for the 25,000 or so people who call the town home.

As a break from the long Alaska Highway, I'm staying for a few days at a nice bed and breakfast just north of town along the Klondike Highway, one that allows dogs.

Its big upper-story windows look out on an endless canopy of boreal forest, thick with an ancientness that seems to radiate outwards—and which is probably also thick with bears.

Here in town by the river, sitting on a bench in the cold mist with Cassie and Weezee at my feet, we're surrounded by the voices of the break-up, and as we wait for the sun's warmth to clear the mists, I recall other voices, those of the breakfast conversation earlier this morning at the B&B.

The cook, Thomas, sets a plate of scrambled eggs in front of me, saying, "I collected the eggs this morning and found one had the beginnings of a chick in it."

"That's not supposed to happen with no rooster," replies his girlfriend Emily, sitting next to me at the big round wooden table. "Looks like the neighbors are letting theirs run again. It'll soon be wolf bait."

I'm not much for eggs in the first place, and now they seem downright unappealing. I drink my orange juice and fiddle with the eggs as the couple answers my questions about the B&B.

"We're filling in for the owner, Ursula, while she's gone to Fort St. John to get supplies to rebuild camp," says Emily. "We're from Vancouver and were on a delivery, but she asked us to stay a few days and help her out."

"A delivery?"

"Yes, we have a seafood business. We bring fresh seafood to Whitehorse twice a month," replies Thomas.

"Where's her camp?" I ask.

"About 20 miles east as the crow flies. Usually she takes a float plane in, but next time she goes in she'll take a crew and a string of pack horses, since they have to rebuild the interior of the cabin and restock everything."

"What happened?" I ask, nibbling on a piece of toast.

Thomas answers, "A grizzly broke in late last fall. Destroyed everything. Shredded the entire cabin, then broke out windows, you name it, just totaled whatever it could."

"I think it has to be the same one that killed the woman down by Teslin," adds Emily.

"Teslin's a good 160 kilometers away," Thomas says doubtfully. "That would be a bit of a hike for a bear."

"No," replies Emily. "Not at all. Grizzlies can range up to 2500 kilometers. Besides, it was actually near Johnson's Crossing, which is only 128 kilometers from here."

Thomas is quiet, seemingly digesting this bit of information.

"128 kilometers, let's see, that's about 80 miles," I comment. "And 2500 kilometers is around 1500 miles."

I think of Janie. "How far are the Chugach Mountains from Whitehorse?" I ask.

Thomas looks perplexed. "You mean in Alaska? Probably at least 700 kilometers, about 350 miles straight west as the crow flies. Why do you ask?"

"Could that same bear have killed someone in the Chugach?" I ask.

Emily answers, "Possible, but unlikely."

"If a bear has a range of over 1,000 miles, it could easily make it to the Chugach, Emily," Thomas replies.

Emily answers, "Yes, but they'd have to climb some huge mountains and cross dangerous glaciers. It wouldn't be easy. I mean, we're talking Kluane National Park—Mount Logan at almost 6 kilometers, over 19,000 feet, plus impassable glaciers."

"It could follow the riverways. That's what the old-time prospectors did," replies Thomas.

We all sit in silence, then I ask, "What happened down at Johnson's Crossing?"

Thomas replies, "It was out on the South Canol Road. A grizzly broke into a cabin where a couple lived—they had moved there from Switzerland to start an adventure business. It was chasing their dog, who ran inside, then the bear broke through a big picture window and chased them both outside. The woman ran and jumped into her car, but the bear started trying to break into it. Her husband had jumped into their other car, and he started honking, which scared the bear off for a moment. The woman didn't have her car keys, so tried to make a break for her husband's car, but as she ran, the bear attacked her. She then played dead as the bear mauled her, which was the wrong thing to do.

Her husband went back inside and got his rifle, then shot the bear. He drove his wife to the Teslin clinic, but she died shortly thereafter."

"It was very tragic," adds Emily, lest I somehow might think otherwise. "We didn't know them, but Ursula did. The whole area's taken it very hard, as they had lots of friends."

I reply with sympathy, "It sounds like a nightmare."

Emily adds, "The reason I wonder if it's not the same bear that ransacked the camp was that the damage to the camp was done only three weeks before the woman was killed. Last October. A bear could easily go 128 kilometers in three weeks. If it was the same bear, it seems it had a chip on its shoulder."

I place my napkin on the table and get up.

"I guess I'll go look around town."

"Would you like me to warm up your eggs?" asks Thomas.

"No thanks, I'm not very hungry."

Emily adds, "Every day, Ursula's dogs go out first thing in the morning and bark their heads off at something down in the valley. One of these days we're going to have the same thing happen here. I'm ready to go back to Vancouver. Just as soon as she comes back, we're gone."

"I understand," I reply. "I'm afraid of bears myself. But it is beautiful here, and I can see why someone would want to live here, bears or no. Thank you for the delicious breakfast. See you later."

Still sitting by the river, I hear the river ice creak and crack even more, and I wonder if bears ever wander into Whitehorse. The mists clear a bit, and I can see a raven resting in a nearby tree, fluffed up against the cold air rising from the Yukon. It's almost noon, and the sun's been up since around 5 a.m., but it's still chilly. Sunset won't come until around 10:30 p.m., after seventeen hours of daylight.

I'm closer than I've ever been to the Land of the Midnight Sun, as Alaska's only a few hours up the road. I've already paid for another night at the B&B, but I'll make my own breakfast tomorrow. No more half-hatched eggs.

Tired of watching the river, I stand, gathering the dogs' leashes. As exhausted as I am from the long drive up through Canada, I'm already wishing we were back on the road.

I head back to my truck, dogs trailing behind. Seeing a little grocery, I tie the dogs and go inside, pleasantly surprised at their stock of fresh fruits and vegetables, as well as gourmet cheeses and teas. I buy enough for several days on the road, as well as some cooked turkey for the dogs.

We'll go somewhere and have a picnic, maybe across the river on Long Lake Road, which the couple at the B&B said was a nice drive on the hillside above town.

I fill my gas tank, then, instead of crossing the Yukon to go to Long Lake, I'm soon going the opposite direction on Robert Service Way, climbing up from the river valley to the intersection with the Alaska Highway.

I'll return to the B&B, get my stuff, and head for Alaska. Maybe they'll give me a refund for tonight, but if not, it's OK—I want to get going.

But as the light at the intersection turns green, I instead impulsively turn south, not north.

Somehow, I need to go to the Canol Road. I know that the road, built in the 1940s, cuts through the heart of grizzly country, and for some reason, the bear story I just heard at the B&B has stirred up disturbing and dark feelings. Maybe there's something I can learn there about Janie's death, even if it's just a better look into my inner self.

I head southeast on the Alaska Highway, retracing my path from the previous day. I'll be at Johnson's Crossing by mid-afternoon and still have hours of daylight. I can drive part way up the Canol Road and still be back at the B&B by dark.

The dogs are soon sleeping to the hum of the truck's engine, and I now wish I'd retrieved my stuff from the B&B so I could just keep going south, back to the desert, back to my ravens and rocks and my wandering. I'm once again questioning the sanity of this ill-conceived mission to find something I can't even define.

As I near Johnson's Crossing, a sense of foreboding returns, and I begin to suspect that there's more to the story of the woman killed by the bear, though I have no logical reason for my suspicions.

Those suspicions will be confirmed when I return to Whitehorse, though that return will be somewhat later than originally planned.

ARCTODUS SIMUS

I kneel and put my hand inside a huge print in the snow alongside the Canol Road, then quickly pull back, as if the very act of touching it will make the bear reappear.

I'm astonished at the size of the bear's pads, not to mention the length of the claw marks. It's the first grizzly print I've ever seen, and its depth and size indicate it's a very large animal.

Standing next to the prints, I slowly sink into the ooze, then step back and examine my boot prints next to that of the grizzly. The average male grizzly weighs 500 pounds, and this one looks to be above average, as its prints are at least five times deeper than mine.

The toes of the tracks are close together, the sides touching each other, and there are clear impressions of long claws. Definitely a grizz, for the toes of the black bear are set farther apart, and blackies have short claws which often don't leave impressions. I've seen lots of black bear tracks in the mountains of Utah and Colorado, and none had this effect on me.

I stand and look around, but I can't see into the thick woods that line both sides of the one-lane dirt road.

The Canol Road (short for Canadian American Norman Oil Line) is all that's left of the effort during WWII by American troops to build a pipeline from Norman Wells for the construction of the Alaska Highway. It's a narrow dirt road that snakes a good 140 miles from Johnson's Crossing to the small town of Ross River, where it meets the Campbell Highway, then continues on to Norman Wells.

The section I'm on is technically called the South Canol Road, while the section continuing on from Ross River is the North Canol Road.

The road is closed in the winter, and it looks as if it's only recently been opened, with mud and patches of snow along its sides.

I've passed several driveways that swing back into the thick stands of poplar and black pine, but was unable to see where they led, though I know one of the drives has to go to the cabin where the woman was killed.

But I'm now apparently beyond all habitation, as I haven't seen any driveways for a good five miles, all of it rough going with potholes and melting snowpack creating occasional mud bogs.

Now, standing here by the grizzly tracks, I quickly realize how fresh they are, as the snow is rapidly melting, changing their contours even as I watch. The bear must have been using the road to travel, avoiding the deeper crusted snow. It may have heard me coming and deviated off into the woods. As fresh as these tracks seem to be, for all I know it could be standing a mere 50 feet away in the thick forest, watching me.

I wonder what it would be like being killed by a bear, and I suddenly turn cold. Sometimes we know how we're going to die, such as when sick with disease, and a bear mauling would also be one of those times—we would know how our end would come about, though we might unfortunately have too much time to think about it.

I jump back into the truck, then sit and eat a granola bar, followed by hot tea from my thermos, filled at the B&B, which now seems far away.

As I sit and think, melancholy sets in. I try to dissuade it, but it's now sitting in the truck cab, squeezing Cassie and Weezee up against me.

"I'm very disappointed in you," it informs me in a quiet voice.

"So am I," I answer agreeably.

"You always pride yourself on feeling comfortable in the wilderness—in fact, you make a case for it being your one true home—but now that you're in true untouched real wilderness, you're shaking like a scared rabbit."

I nod again. "Guilty as charged. In fact, more than guilty, as any place there's a road, it's not even true wilderness, so I would be even worse way out there. You've made your point and can now leave anytime you wish."

Melancholy leaves and fear slips in and takes its place, as I think I see something dark moving in the trees lining the road, exactly where the bear tracks enter the forest. I start the truck and back around.

Time to go.

Yes, I've learned something by coming here, something I would perhaps rather not know. I wanted a better look into my inner self, but I'm not sure I like what I see.

The Pleistocene hunters who once inhabited this area thousands of years ago would have been incredulous to see how afraid a fellow human can be even when surrounded by relative safety.

Here I sit, in the warmth and security of my truck—something they could never have conceived of even in their wildest dreams—and I'm scared of a bit of movement in the forest. It seems we humans have gone a bit soft, or at least I'm not the adventurer I had thought I was. Even the First Nations people who now inhabit this region, people such as the Tlingits in Teslin, would think I was pathetic.

I'll go back to Whitehorse, gather my stuff, and head south, back home, wherever home is. It seems that since Janie was killed, I've become more and more fearful, even out in the deserts of Utah, where there's really nothing to be afraid of.

As I start back down the road towards Johnson's Crossing, I'm suddenly spinning out. I put the truck in compound gear and try to slowly inch my way out of the mud, but the wheels just continue to spin and sink deeper. I try rocking the track back-and-forth, but to no avail.

I'm stuck. The day has warmed up enough that the snow is rapidly melting, water now running onto the road like a small stream, and it's all become a big mud bog.

I get out, sinking into mud up to my ankles, then slide my way to the edge of the road, wiping my feet off on the yellow grasses. I collect as many large sticks as I can carry, wading back into the mud and cramming them under my rear tires.

I do this over and over, until I've created a type of corduroy road, just like that which underlies the sections of the Alaska Highway that go over permafrost, though the road builders there used large logs.

Back in the truck, I gradually ease my way forward until the truck sinks again at the end of my little wooden bridge. Stuck again.

This whole time, I've been keeping an eye on the woods on the other side of the road, where I saw the movement. My feet are soaked and cold, so I climb back into the truck and take off my boots and socks. I crank up the heater and try to dry out while drinking more tea.

The dogs now need a break, so I let them briefly get out, then make them get quickly back in. They're now covered with mud, as is the seat of the truck. I get out and again haul as many small logs as I can, repeating the process, but this time, the truck doesn't budge even an inch.

It's now twilight, a time that seems to last forever in the spring and summer of the far North. And once night does come, it's not really very dark, as the sun never goes very far below the horizon. Arctic darkness is more like dusk in most places.

It's starting to get cold, so I change into my warm clothes—long johns, fleece top and bottoms, down jacket, and wool socks—and pull my down sleeping bag out of the back, as well as bags for the dogs. I feed them some more turkey, along with some biscuits and water, then take them out again. They seem nervous and are soon wanting back into the truck.

Is something out there, or are my fears feeding theirs?

I drink the last of my hot tea, then prepare for a long night. Fortunately, my gas tank is almost full, so I can turn the truck on long enough to run the heater for short periods if it gets too cold.

As I sit there, thinking about the dark form I saw earlier, the fact that I'm truly on my own begins to sink in. The Canol Road, other than serving the few houses near Johnson's Crossing, is used only by more adventurous tourists or an occasional driver from Ross River on their way to Whitehorse. The odds are good that I could sit here for days, maybe weeks, before being discovered, especially this early in the season. I know I'll probably have to walk out in the morning.

As night falls, I become acutely aware of my predicament. I think of the many stories of people who have died unprepared in the northern wilds—many books have been written about their adventures and bad luck.

Not far from where I'm stuck are immense stretches of true wilderness and vast mountain ranges with peaks not only unnamed but also untouched, places like the Cirque of the Unclimbables. I picture glaciers that stretch forever, their rough surfaces broken by yawning crevasses hidden by crusted snow.

I think of the young man who fell through such a crevasse three hundred years ago and was wedged upright until his body was found recently by sheep hunters, only a hundred miles west of here in the Tatshenshini-Alsek Provincial Wilderness Park of British Columbia.

A torrent of water melting from the glacier exposed his frozen remains, dressed in a cloak of arctic ground squirrel pelts, his belongings strewn nearby: a finely woven broad-brimmed hat, a walking stick, a spear, and a leather pouch containing edible leaves and fish.

Archaeologists named the 20-year-old man Kwaday Dan Ts'inchi, which means "long-ago person found" in the southern Tutchone language, a language that's part of the Athabaskan family, as is Navajo. The region where he was found is part of the traditional territory of the Champagne and Aishihik First Nations.

After the scientists studied Kwaday Dan, First Nations members cremated his remains and spread them with ceremony across the glacier where he'd been found. DNA testing showed the iceman to be an ancestor of a number of nearby First Nations people.

Unlike Kwaday Dan, my likelihood of dying out here really isn't that high, I figure, as I can always walk out to the highway in the morning. Now settled down onto the truck's bench seat, doors locked, dogs cuddled against me, I finally drift off to sleep.

I dream that I'm sitting on a rocky ridge high above an endless blue glacier, watching as a young black-haired man dressed in fur pelts walks far below on the glacier's ragged slopes.

He suddenly falls into a crevasse and is gone, and I wake with a startle.

Disoriented, it takes a moment to remember where I am. I then realize what actually woke me—something is walking around the truck, something big, and now it's pushing against the truck as if trying to get inside.

I sit up, terrified, encumbered by my sleeping bag as I hunt in the dark for my bear spray. The dogs growl.

Now I hear what sounds like the scraping of long claws across the hood. An image of a Pleistocene dire bear,

Arctodus simus, fills my half-asleep consciousness like a dream—an adult Arctodus simus could reach 12 feet in height and weigh nearly a ton.

Panicked, I turn on the truck, honking the horn as I put it in first and step on the accelerator. Like before, the truck spins out, but suddenly, wheels find traction and the truck lunges forward. The mud has frozen, giving me a reprieve.

As I drive away, wheels crunching on the frozen mud, my headlights reveal the startled form of a large bull moose, his nubby spring antlers in velvet. He stands motionless in shock for a moment, then turns and bolts into the trees. Later, I find scrape marks from his teeth along the hood of my truck.

I'm soon rolling along the Alaska Highway in the dark towards Whitehorse, watching for woods bison on the road, where they sometimes sleep on the relative warmth of the pavement, hard to spot, as their eyes don't reflect light.

Before long, I'm back at the B&B, where I slip quietly into my room and settle into the comfort and security of my warm bed, dogs at my feet—happily home, if only for the short remainder of the night.

AN ABSOLUTE, CATASTROPHIC COLLISION OF EVENTS

The next morning, I gather my stuff and say goodbye to my hosts, then head back into town, stopping at a small restaurant for breakfast. There, I notice a newspaper on a table and pick it up, drawn in by the headline: "Shocking Discovery about Teslin Woman Killed by Bear." I sit down with a cup of coffee and cinnamon roll and read:

A coroner's inquest of a woman who died last fall from a bear mauling near Teslin has revealed a strange and tragic set of circumstances. The bear, who had chased the woman and her husband from their cabin, was mauling the woman when her husband shot it twice, killing it.

Though the husband immediately took his wife to the Teslin clinic, they couldn't save her, and she died shortly thereafter. Because the woman was severely mauled, the clinic doctor failed to see the true cause of her death. Investigators have now determined that a third bullet ricocheted off a nearby tree and struck the woman in the chest.

Kirsten Macdonald, Yukon's chief coroner, said, "What transpired at that property on that day was an absolute, catastrophic collision of events."

I lean back in my chair, amazed. The husband's picture is next to the story, and he looks truly devastated. He is, of course, innocent, as the inquest has shown, for no one can intentionally direct a ricocheted bullet to a given destination.

He was trying to save his wife and instead, killed her. He had become the lead actor in a story more poignant than any Shakespearean tragedy.

The article continues:

The investigators reported finding a single poker chip glued to the bear's fur. It is believed that the animal ransacked a camp three weeks before killing the woman, broke open a bottle of glue and accidentally glued a poker chip to itself.

The cook's girlfriend had been right. This was most likely the same bear that had devastated their hunting camp. The bear definitely had a chip on its shoulder, both literally and figuratively.

An editorial accompanies the article:

Death by bear is probably one of the most brutal ways a human can die. This tragedy underscores the need for better education about what to do in a bear attack, as the woman played dead when she should have fought, as the bear was acting predatory. Playing dead with a predatory bear doesn't work. One must fight. One plays dead only when the attacking bear has cubs.

I sip my coffee, thinking of the horrors of being mauled by a grizzly, of what Janie must have gone through, my hesitation to continue north growing with each moment.

Will my own search for Janie's killer end in similar tragedy? Will people say I should have stayed home? Will they shake their heads at how my own fate transpired?

I know logically that my actions may lead to my own destruction, yet something in me keeps pushing, some sort of compulsion.

I'm soon in my truck once again heading north, knowing that the heart will defy all logic to find what it most needs.

THE WOLVES OF NAHANNI

Continuing north, I think of how my grandfather told me that once you've been to the north country you can never forget it. He drove to Alaska every summer, buying a new pickup in the Lower 48 and selling it in Fairbanks, making enough to pay for his trip up and subsequent flight back to Colorado.

I can still hear his voice, telling my mom and dad about his latest trip over morning coffee while I sipped hot chocolate, listening, taking it all in as only a kid can do.

"You never forget the light, the way the sun always shines at an odd angle, the sight of fields of fireweed in bloom, the intangible quality of a whole different way of life. The North has something unique and indescribable about it. It embodies the spirit of adventure."

But I also remember Gramps saying, "It might be better not to ever go up there, as it does kind of haunt you. You end up thinking about it way too much, wanting to go back. It makes you feel unsettled, even if you're home, where you know you want to be."

Like me, Gramps was a desert rat, yet he always felt the pull of the north country and seemed destined to spend his summers driving up the Alcan, now called the Alaska

Highway. He would always have a wistful look on his face when he returned from Alaska and talked about his trip endlessly, even though he said he was glad to be home.

And now, here I am, in the North. Will I, too, be destined to come back again and again, leaving behind my ravens and redrock and endless open vistas, instead surrounded by thick boreal forest laced with ancient bear trails?

Once, after hearing Gramps talk about Alaska, I had a dream where my parents had decided to move to Fairbanks. I frantically protested, saying, "But there's no redrock there. What will I do?"

I awoke, and realizing I was in my own bedroom back home, I felt a deep sense of relief, though the unsettled feeling lingered. Even though I was just a kid, I vowed never to go to the North Country.

Not far north of Whitehorse, I drive past a couple who have parked their motorhome by the highway and are walking their dogs, two black labs. I think of Moki, of her sweet face, and all feels lost.

I suddenly miss the desert, the hot sun, the cool shady cottonwood groves along canyon streams, the firecracker penstemon and canyon sweetpea, the lyrical call of the canyon wren, and Moki's sweet whimper when I would break out the hotdogs around the campfire.

I'm soon 30 miles from Whitehorse in the Ibex Valley, where wild horses run free and free wolves run wild. I think back to the cabin in Colorado where I left the door open and invited the wolves in—I'm not so sure I would do that here, as they might just take me up on the offer.

Most residents of Whitehorse keep their dogs indoors at night in the winter so wolves won't kill them. In the summer, the wolves can find meals out in the wilds, so generally stay away. Wolves tend to pack up more in the winter, when the power of numbers can make a moose kill more profitable. A pack of 15 or 20 isn't unheard of.

Soon, I pass through Haines Junction, where I toy with the idea of going to the small Alaskan village of Haines, famous for bear-watching in the autumn when the bears come down to the Chilkat River to fish for salmon alongside bald eagles, who prefer trout. Haines can be reached only by going through Canada, unless you choose to visit by water. Instead, I continue north into the reaches of half-frozen Kluane Lake.

To me, Kluane Country is one of the most beautiful landscapes on Earth. The lofty white peaks of the St. Elias Mountains of Kluane National Park stand to the west, beckoning me to a land I'll never know, the land of Mt. Logan, Canada's highest peak at 19,551 feet and with a prominence of 17,220 feet. Mt. Logan also has the largest base circumference of any non-volcanic mountain on Earth.

The peak was first climbed by non-natives in 1925, when an international team of climbers crossed the Canada mainland from the Pacific coast by train, then walked the remaining 120 miles to the Logan Glacier where they established base camp. Most of today's adventurers would never even conceive of such a trip.

It's through this country, Kluane Country, that the grizzly that killed Janie would have had to travel to reach Whitehorse, but the bear wouldn't have had the luxury of going partway by train.

We reach the southern terminus of the lake, crossing a bridge where the icy blue meltwaters from the Kaskawulsh Glacier feed the deeper blue waters of the lake.

I'm soon at historic mile 1061, Soldiers' Summit, where the Alaska Highway was officially opened on November 20, 1942, at a temperature of minus 35 degrees.

I think back to camping on Soldier Summit in Utah, to what seems like years ago, where I stood in the night and pondered my future while gazing at the folds of the Milky Way. Then, the thought of going north to the land of polar bears and blue glacier bears seemed half lunacy, half sane. Time will tell which half makes up the whole story.

Paralleling the lake, we're soon at the tiny village of Destruction Bay, named for a fierce wind that hit in the 1940s, destroying everything.

I stop for gas, and while filling up, a small heavy-set man filling a motorhome at the next pump asks, "Seen any bears? There's supposed to be lots of them around this part of the Yukon."

We talk for a moment, and he informs me he's already seen four bears between here and Whitehorse.

"They like to feed on the grasses and tubers along the highway this time of year. We saw three black bears and one grizzly. They pay you no mind, and we stopped and got lots of good video."

He pulls out ahead of me, and I note he has Alberta plates—Wildrose Country. I suddenly long to be on a farm west of Calgary in the rolling hills, wild mountains in the far distance, free of thoughts of death by bear, even though the prairies were once prime grizzly range. I recall seeing a sign on my way up along the highway north of Edmonton that read, "The Grizzly Trail."

Now north of Destruction Bay, I see my first sign for Fairbanks—692 kilometers, or about 430 miles. I'll turn left once I reach Alaska and go back south long before Fairbanks, going to Palmer, near the Chugach Mountains, just north of Anchorage. I'll use the town as my base camp, but base camp for what, I don't yet know.

I meet an occasional vehicle going south and feel the tug I've been fighting all the way up here. I can almost hear Gramps' voice: "Turn around and go home—you'll be sorry if you don't." But Gramps would have never told me that, so it must be someone else's voice—probably that of my own internal fears.

I see a smudge of brown against the green pines and quickly pull over onto the highway shoulder. There, grazing on the sedges along the road is a brown-colored bear. I slowly pull forward until I'm right alongside it, though it's still a good 40 feet back near the edge of the trees.

Cassie and Weezee look out the passenger window, eyes wide, as the bear continues to browse, totally ignoring us. It has a hump on its powerful shoulders, muscle that helps it dig—a grizzly.

Could this be the bear that killed Janie? I know the odds are infinitesimal, and yet I can't help but be fascinated by the thick jaws that rip grasses from the ground. It's close enough that I can see its long claws, prized for First Nations necklaces.

Bears are omnivores, with berries and vegetation making up the greatest part of their diet, though they crave protein in the fall when they put on fat for winter hibernation. Here, up north, salmon fit the bill quite well. In fact, fall can be the best time to see bears, as they're so busy eating they'll ignore humans—that is, unless you're the only food around.

After taking a number of photos, I drive on, feeling like I just witnessed something very special. I wonder how many bears Canada has, though I'm sure nobody knows for sure, which is as it should be.

I'm eventually in Beaver Creek, the last settlement in the Yukon on the Alaska Highway before entering Alaska. I'll cross the border in a few miles, and I decide to stop and take a break—not that the border crossing will take long, but somehow the idea of finally reaching Alaska has taken on a mythic feeling, like I'm on the crux of something that will forever alter my life, if not perhaps end it. Might be safer to stay here in the wild Yukon.

A few miles out of town, I pull off onto what looks like an old forestry road, overgrown with some kind of currant bushes, tiny pink blossoms crowning the ends of the stems, precursors to berries for autumn bear feasts. Finding a wide spot, I turn around, then get out, yelling, "Hey bear, hey moose." I listen for a moment, then let the dogs out.

Cassie and Weezee instantly have their hackles up, peering into the thick shrubbery next to the road. I immediately think of bears. If it were a moose, the dogs wouldn't try to make themselves look larger as a defense, the purpose of hackles, but would instead want to chase.

I tell them to get back into the truck, which they immediately do, somewhat to my surprise. Waiting, ready to get back in the truck myself, I'm curious to see what they smelled.

To my surprise, a head pokes from the bushes, a head with big bold intelligent eyes, thick jaws, and a silvery-gray coat. Its mouth is full of something gray and fluffy, and I quickly realize it's a wolf carrying a dead rabbit. I should have yelled, "Hey wolf."

It had probably just killed the rabbit before we drove in and interrupted its lunch, but it seems good natured about it all as it stands and watches us with big yellow eyes.

"Hello, wolf, sorry to bother you," I say softly, and it quickly turns and disappears back into the shrubs. It appears to be a good 70 or 80 pounds, powerful and athletic.

Getting back into the truck I sit for awhile, trying to take in what I've just seen—not just my first wolf in the wild, but my first wolf ever.

For a moment I feel as if something's lost, some long-gone interconnectedness that disappeared when my species chose to try to remove predators from the planet. I feel sad, and yet, given my own fears, I understand how one might feel with wild terrifying beasts ready to take away one's children and livestock.

And yet, wolves have killed very few people, much fewer than bears and mountain lions. Our main enemy is other humans, who have killed millions of our kind, whereas predators such as bears have killed very few of us in comparison. It's a paradox, an irrational fear, our night terror of wild animals, a fear we should reserve for one another.

I think of Joanne Ronan Moore, who spent almost a year with her husband John in the wilderness of Nahanni

National Park in the 1970s building a cabin and reveling in the quiet and beauty of deep winter in the Yukon.

She writes in her book, *Nahanni Trailhead*, of wolves coming to their cabin and peering through the windows, trying to dig in through the logs, and shredding their laundry hanging outside, as well as carrying off an axe. The couple finally took to sleeping in the loft of their cabin for safety, pulling the ladder up behind them.

Before they finally left, winter over, the Moores one day found themselves out away from the safety of the cabin, where they were graced by the sight of a pack of almost 30 wolves.

The couple watched in fascination as two silver wolves stood on a bank as if on guard as the entire pack walked by. The two guard wolves then fell in at the rear and followed the pack. A final wolf walked by the Moores and barked at them like a dog, then ran away.

Nahanni National Park is some distance away, but, like bears, wolves can range far and wide, and as I drive away, I wonder if the wolf I saw could be an offspring of one of the Nahanni wolves.

Does it, too, have its own story, carried in the scent of its fur, its worn claws and teeth—a story of moose meat, distant horizons, deep forests, and dens of pups? Does it have a sense of place, of home?

I'm soon at the border station for Alaska, the only vehicle there, and the border guard is pleasant, asking for my passport and welcoming me back to the United States. It seems odd to be back home in a place I've never been, but I suddenly feel that sense of security one has when in a familiar culture. It seems incredibly handy to no longer have to translate kilometers into miles, and the road seems much better maintained with fewer frost heaves.

Will I see wolves in Alaska?

But as the border station fades in the rear-view mirror, everything still looks the same, and I wonder if the station wasn't an illusion and I'm somehow still in Canada.

I turn off the Alaska Highway at the town of Tok, named for housing the many Japanese workers from Tokyo during the highway's construction. I'm now on the Glenn Highway, flanked by stunning views of the Wrangell Mountains in the distance, some of which are active volcanoes. The Wrangells eventually make way for the Chugach, equally distant, like something in one's dreamy imagination.

What was an illusive plan is now becoming real, and soon I'll be at my destination in the town of Palmer, in the shadow of the Chugach, where bears can sit and gaze down upon the town from the high flanks of Pioneer Peak.

THE LOST LAND OF BERINGIA

I still have several hundred miles before I reach Palmer, and since I'm paralleling the distant mountains, they seem to never change, impressive with their snowy untouched peaks on the far horizon.

I think again of *Horribilis*, wondering if it had indeed crossed these mighty mountains after killing Janie. I know it's vastly unlikely, given the massive peaks and glaciers it would have had to navigate, but it wouldn't be the first to cross such uncharted terrain.

Early nomads migrated through this region ten thousand years ago during the Late Pleistocene, possibly even earlier. Parts of Alaska and much of the Yukon were never glaciated during the Ice Age, allowing animals and humans alike passage while the rest of Canada and parts of Alaska were buried under glaciers a mile thick.

The ice-free part of Alaska and the Yukon were part of what's called Beringia, that region surrounding the Bering Strait and the Chukchi and Bering seas. It included parts of Russia as well as Alaska and Canada, and because the Ice Age resulted in shallower oceans, the Bering Land Bridge, approximately 620 miles wide, allowed for migration between Siberia and North America.

Glaciers never formed in Beringia because the climate was too dry—there wasn't enough snowfall. The region was a grassland steppe, and the giant mammals of the Ice Age flourished there—the mastodon, steppe bison, scimitar cat, and giant short-faced bear, among others.

Archaeological evidence shows that humans crossed the bridge many years ago, possibly following the hefty meals that came with successful hunts of large mammals like mastodons and bison. Cut bones have been found in the Yukon's Arctic that have been carbon dated to 25,000 years and older.

Archaeologists have long thought the extinction of many of the Pleistocene species were the result of over-hunting by humans, but newer radiocarbon dates on mastodon (Mammut americanum) fossils in Alaska and Yukon suggest that this species was locally extinct tens of thousands of years before humans crossed the bridge. However, recent excavations have found evidence of humans in the region some 45,000 years ago, so the extinction theory can now be revived, assuming the dating is correct.

Before European colonization, Beringia was inhabited on both sides of the bridge by the Yupik peoples. These nomadic hunters spoke the Athabaskan language (Dene), and evidence of their nomadic nature lies with the Navajo and Apache in the Southwest, who speak forms of Athabaskan that are remarkably similar to that spoken by the Yukon's First Nations peoples, despite centuries of separation.

I think of Kwaday Dan Ts'inchi and wonder how close his lifestyle was to that of his ancestors. I suspect not much had changed through the years, not until the invasion of the Europeans.

Much of Beringia is now a lost land, vanished undersea in the meltwaters of the end of the last Ice Age, though parts of it can still be found in northern and central Yukon, Alaska and Siberia.

Do the Yupik, the native peoples who still hunt these great landscapes, have stories that reshape their own pasts, that reweave learned lessons into words that can help others live their best lives, make their best hunts? Do their histories tell of crossing the great land bridge, or are such tales lost in time?

Do they tell stories of hope, of authenticity, of what it means to be a human on a spinning planet in a place of long summer days where magic appears in the night skies? Now non-nomadic, do they feel at home, their wandering days over, or do their hearts feel heavy, haunted by past motion? Do they tell tales reflecting a deep need to wander?

It was late fall when the bear killed Janie, a time when it should have been in hibernation, though the Chugach area isn't as cold as more northern Alaska. But by then, the bears are typically in their long winter sleep, a metabolic process that's not well understood. And in the last few weeks of autumn they desperately try to find calories to help them survive the winter.

The brown bears fishing at the famous Brooks Falls in Katmai National Park in southern Alaska have been known to eat 40,000-plus salmon calories a day. These bears can weigh over 1000 pounds, yet are mere one-pound cubs when born in the den, their moms still in hibernation—the cubs crawl to the pap to nurse while mom sleeps.

But those seasons when the berries don't ripen and food is scarce, hungry bears come down into what used to be their prime habitat before we humans made it ours. They rampage through our garbage cans, and some even come inside our houses, desperately hungry.

Even though Davie thought Janie startled the bear or that it might have had cubs, I often wonder if the grizzly that killed her was hungry—or maybe just tired of it all, tired of the ubiquitous humans everywhere.

AURORA

And now, this far north, the days have become much longer. I finally stop, and even though it's late, it's still daylight, though the sun is low, reflecting alpenglow off the huge Matanuska Glacier in the distance.

I'm not far from Palmer, and I pull off the highway into a large gravel pit, source of winter road sand for this portion of the highway.

I feed the dogs, get out a camp chair, then relax, a can of soup warming on my little stove. The dogs are happy to stretch their legs but don't go far, maybe thinking of wolves. We're surrounded by a thick forest of fir and larch trees.

I retrace my journey so far, then for some unknown reason my thoughts drift to the desert I've left far behind.

I drift back to a time when I lived in a house in a small desert town, years ago in my youth. I'm suddenly wandering the streets in my mind's eye, and it's almost as if I'm there, for I can see all the places that once formed the frame of my life—the house I lived in with its small back deck looking out to distant mesas across miles of slickrock, heirloom lilac bushes lining the flagstone pathway to the back gate, a gate that opened into coyote territory. White sandstone fins and whalebacks stretched into the infinity of geologic time, my own time a mere blink of an eye. A trail led out into the wilds, beckoning, and I recall the many times I walked that trail, times that layer deeper and deeper into a lifetime.

A cracking sound from the trees at the edge of the gravel pit brings me back to the present, back to the northern forest lands, lands so different from my beloved desert. Dogs' ears are perked, but nothing emerges from the trees, and all is quiet—probably just a moose.

We're now far enough north that the deer have turned into moose. Moose are members of the deer family and can live further north than deer, who are limited in their range.

A warming climate is bringing many changes to the Arctic regions, including moose spreading farther and farther north, following the shrubs that are now able to grow there. Other changes are afoot, including the interbreeding of grizzly and polar bears, as grizzly territory is expanding while polar bear territory is contracting, giving the grizzly an edge. Did the bear that killed Janie carry polar bear DNA?

I think of all these changes around me and suddenly I'm tired. Soon a sadness prevails, and as night finally falls and the shadows lengthen, a full-blown feeling of sorrow hits me hard.

I'm missing Moki.

What is it about our genetic makeup that makes us feel such sorrow even when there's nothing we can do about it?

Death of those we love makes us more aware of our mortality, of the ticking of the clock, the moments of our lives passing. And why are some stuck in the past, reliving it over and over in memories? Is it a substitute for the uncertainty of the future? Or is it a refusal to create anything new, trying to force the present into the future?

And so, I gradually let it all slip through my fingers, through my mind, day by day of my past, until it's gone forever, while sitting there in my camp chair somewhere in a gravel pit in Alaska.

The desert was once my home, but now it seems as if nowhere is home—or is it everywhere? And why exactly do I need a home? Home seems to be a mental construct, an intangible emotion held only in the mind, something not really real.

Our hunter-gatherer ancestors must have found the concept of home to be quite foreign. Their idea of home had to have been many places, a geographic range, like other large mammals have, and I suspect our ancestors would have found the concept of home as being only one static place an unmanageable reality.

They would probably have been aghast if made to stay in one place. What would they eat after everything had been depleted? It was a necessity to roam, how they survived. Only after agriculture was invented, a mere 6,000 years ago, were people able to stay in one place.

But there are also reversals in nomadism, as illustrated by the Plains tribes, who gave up a more sedentary way of life for one of movement after the Spanish introduced the horse.

Is death the ultimate home? The one place where we no longer worry about food, shelter, comfort, security? Some long for death, for its finality. Those who don't believe in an afterlife perhaps have the ultimate comfort in the thought of death, for one simply ceases to be. No more needs or wants or desires, no more painful memories, no more nostalgia, no more happiness, no more anything, just the ultimate reunion of our molecules with those of the universe, our ultimate home.

Did Janie find her true home? Did the bear save her from years of some unknown grief she might have otherwise suffered? Would she have chosen to live had she known she was going to die of some painful disease? Even most who know they're dying hang on as long as possible, for most of us fear death, no matter how fearless we imagine ourselves to be.

It's now dark, and I've made up our beds in the truck, dogs cozied down into their warm sleeping bags, the nights still cold up here where winter desperately tries to hold on, to not die.

I pause for a moment before crawling into the cab, and just then the sky begins to dance to the north in shades of green and yellow and even purple—the Northern Lights, or Aurora Borealis.

The aurora finally fades, and I crawl into the truck and tuck myself into my sleeping bag. But just as I begin to drift off, I feel as if something's hanging above me, and I open my eyes to see a red glow all around as if the sun were rising, even though it's only midnight.

I step out of the truck again, transfixed by what looks like alpenglow on the distant Chugach Mountains, glowing burgundy far on the horizon.

The aurora's back, even brighter than before, and now the sky begins a slow dance, huge undulating curtains of reds and maroons, the rarest of auroral colors, caused when electrons strike oxygen atoms at higher altitudes, which happens only during intense solar activity.

I later discover that the word aurora comes from the Latin aurea, meaning golden or gleaming like gold, but this aurora seems more like a red dragon's breath.

I now feel as if Janie's here with me—I feel her sense of wonder and love of life. This is followed by the realization and poignancy that she's gone, and that instead I'm the one who gets to experience life in this rarest form. For some reason, I think she would have felt it deeper and loved it more, felt more at home here in this land of her birth.

A month or so before she died, Janie was once again trying to talk me into settling down, into finding a place where I could find stability and maybe even put down roots. She worried about me that way, she and Davie both.

"Chinle," Janie said, "It's important to feel like you belong to a place, to stay somewhere long enough to create memories, to get to know people who you can belong to, who know and understand you. Connections can make you happy, you know."

"I get bored," I replied. "I can't help it, Janie, one minute I'm happy and the next I need to go someplace different."

"It's kind of a curse, isn't it?" she asked gently, then added, "But at least you don't get stuck in one place, like I've managed to do."

"I thought you loved Hawaii."

"I do, but I miss Alaska sometimes—the glaciers and big peaks and the wildness of it all. And Utah, too—the blackbrush and redrock."

Ironically, if Janie had stayed in Hawaii, she would still be alive. But who knows, maybe not, maybe something bad would have happened there. We can never predict where our lives will end up—or just end.

The day after that conversation, I collected some colorful rocks and several blackbrush stems and carefully wrapped them and mailed them to Janie.

I can still hear her laughter when she called to tell me it was the best gift she'd ever received.

SHE WHO WALKS LEAVING NO TRACKS

May is the best month for the wildflowers to bloom in the high Utah desert—the aromatic cliffrose, the sand verbena, the tall pink Palmer's penstemon—and I'm homesick, even though I don't have a home.

The gray on Weezee's muzzle seems more pronounced, for on May 1st she turned 14, the average lifespan of a Blue Heeler. That means she will live a few years more, I hope, as averages are made of times shorter and longer.

I've rented an old farm cottage on the outskirts of Palmer, between the Matanuska and Knik rivers, both of which flow from huge glaciers in the Chugach. It's a rural area, and the nearest neighbor is an old grizzled guy who seems to embody Old Alaska, with old tools and junk and moose antlers hanging on the side of his decrepit old shed.

Every time someone drives down the dirt lane, no matter how fast or slow they go, he comes out and shakes his fist at them and yells, "Slow down, you bloody bastards!" Several times in the night I hear gunshots coming from the vicinity of his house and wonder if he's poaching moose.

One day, I return to the farm house to find two Alaska State Troopers leading him from his house in handcuffs, and it's the last I see of him.

Instead of going to where where Janie was killed in the Chugach, my purpose for coming, I've spent the last two weeks driving down to the Kenai Peninsula, going up Hatcher Pass, driving to the town of Talkeetna to see the mighty Denali, and sitting on Bird Point above Turnagain Arm, watching a beluga whale, then the six-foot bore tide rush past at 15 mph. I have yet to hike even one step into the Chugach. For some reason, now that I'm here, it all seems somewhat futile.

What was I thinking? Did I really think I could solve Janie's death by coming up here? And what's there to solve anyway? She startled a bear and it killed her. It's all simple and straightforward. Even though Roddie told me the area where she died, I now have no desire to go there.

Something seems so different about the reality of it all now that I'm here, and I suspect it's exactly that—the reality of it versus my own imaginings. Have I built it all into something mythological with my growing fear of bears?

Alaska is no stranger to death by bear, and maulings are even more common. Anchorage alone has an estimated 300 black bears and 40 to 50 grizzlies—all living in the city limits—and on average, one person a year dies in Alaska from a bear attack. Yet moose are much more dangerous, causing more deaths and injuries than bears.

In 2013 and 2014, the Alaska Department of Fish and Game put GPS collars and video cameras on six black bears and three brown bears, tracking their movements for six weeks. Though bears have plenty of natural foods in Anchorage, they spend their time looking for human food, which they find tastier. All the bears pretty much stayed in the Anchorage area.

One collared black bear was tracked eating a moose leg, then sitting watching a biker. He then went for a swim across Cook Inlet, ate some birdseed from a deck, and had a dinner of seagull eggs. A second black bear raided several chicken coops, boarded a boat, ate dog food from a dish in someone's yard, and then took off with a bag of trash.

Anchorage is bounded to the east by Chugach State Park, a 500,0000-acre wilderness area, home to a large number of black and brown bears, though the exact population is uncertain because no census has ever been conducted. I wonder if the Anchorage bears don't occasionally go visit their wilder neighbors there, kicking back and telling stories of urban life, of gourmet chicken dinners with dog food for dessert.

In spite of the large number of bears in Chugach State Park, there have only been several maulings there over the years.

Finally, one morning, with the same suddenness that hit me when I decided to spread Moki's ashes, I wake and decide it's time to go into the Chugach.

I put together a daypack with snacks and water, walk the dogs, then leave them to their own devices in the farm house, something I rarely do. I hope they'll sleep while I'm gone, but I decide to call the woman I'm renting from to tell her my plan, just in case I don't come back.

I never worry about such things, but this feels different—I've had a sense of foreboding even before coming here, something I can't shake, and I've also had strange dreams nightly, usually a mishmash of bears and Janie and clouds swirling over a full moon that lights up huge otherworldly glacial peaks beckoning me to come climb them.

I say goodbye to Cassie and Weezee, hesitatingly petting their soft noses, and they seem to reflect my trepidation back, as if sensing something's wrong, ignoring the biscuits I've left them.

I drive slowly down the lane, kind of missing being yelled at by the old codger, wondering why he's in jail. I'll have to remember to ask my landlady later when I call to tell her I'm back—assuming I return.

I'm soon on the Old Glenn Highway, following the Knik River, then crossing its wide braided channel. The highway cuts directly across the enormous steep slopes of the base of Pioneer Peak, slopes that drop into the Knik Arm, reminding me of the steep mountains on Oahu, not far from where Janie lived.

I can see mudflats along the water, and I think of a story Janie told me about when she was a kid and her family came to Turnagain Arm to watch the boretides and to picnic.

As they sat above the shore, they watched as someone in an old pickup drove out onto the mudflats. Janie's dad, my Uncle Lynn, worried that they would sink, as the intertidal areas along Turnagain Arm are dangerous, for their seemingly solid surface can suddenly become like quicksand, and people and animals trapped in the mud have drowned in the rapidly rising tides, some despite rescue efforts.

But the truck didn't sink, and its two occupants got out and fished for awhile. From their vantage point, Janie and her family could now see the boretide coming in, and they frantically yelled at the people below them to get out.

It took a few minutes to make them aware of what was going on, and soon the rising water had engulfed the truck's wheels. The pair barely managed to gun the truck out before the full tide hit, and water was all the way up to the truck's bed before they managed to get to higher ground.

I now see the road to Eklutna Lake, my original destination, but I instead opt to go to the nearby 200-foot-tall Thunder Bird Falls, where I park and start up a pleasant trail bordering Eklutna Canyon.

It's an easy trail, only a mile to the falls, but I soon turn back, deterred by the number of people and also recognizing my own attempt to further delay what I came for. I'll see the falls another day.

Janie was killed on the flanks of Eklutna Canyon, but further up. I realize that I'm procrastinating going to where she died. I might just as well turn around and go back to the farm house, gather my stuff and the dogs, and go back to Utah.

I sit in my truck for awhile, then decide to continue on, even though the sense of dread is now stronger. I know I should listen to my intuition—it's served me well in the past—but I'm having trouble deciding if it's really my intuition or just a fear I build up the closer I get.

I head back and take the road that goes up Eklutna Canyon, dead-ending at the Eklutna Campground on the shores of Eklutna Lake. I'm soon on the Eklutna Lake Trail, an easy hike through birch and cottonwood groves along the shores of the lake's mirror-like surface, flanked by the towering Chugach.

I feel a sense of urgency, maybe from not wanting to leave the dogs very long, but possibly from some deep instinct that says to get the task over with and get back to my truck, even though I'm not sure what the task is.

The further I hike, the fewer people I see, until at last, after about four miles, I come to a sign marking the Bold Ridge Trail, which veers away from the lake and up a drainage between Bleak and Bright Peaks.

The trail soon climbs, making me slow my pace, though the sense of urgency is still there. After switchbacking in places through thick timber, the trail takes hold on a ridge going south to Bold Peak. It becomes difficult with loose footing, making me go even slower.

I haven't seen anyone since turning off the main trail, and it looks like I'll soon reach timberline. I wonder if I'll see some sheep, and at times I stop to take in the spectacular views across the valley and of the lake below.

I'm going slower and slower and can now see tundra ahead. I wonder if there are any bears nearby, but it all seems somewhat anticlimactic, here in the real world as opposed to the world of my strange dreams and imaginings.

Looking across a long stretch of tundra, I recall reading somewhere about a place in the Wrangells where bears have created a long path in the tundra, generation after generation using the same trail, stepping in the same footprints of the previous bears, carving long trains of divots in the landscape.

I stop and sit on a rock, drinking water and eating a handful of gorp, wondering how close I am to where Janie died. All I know is that I'm in the general vicinity and that her body was found behind a large rock, as if purposely hidden.

The thought makes me shiver, even though it's a beautiful warm day. The feeling of oppression is now stronger, and I fight the urge to leave, to run.

There's movement ahead, is it a bear? A surge of adrenaline goes straight to my heart, and I quietly hide behind a large block of volcanic rock, maybe even the same rock that Janie had hid behind, if she'd indeed been hiding.

I hear the crunch of footsteps and realize that soft bear paws don't crunch—it can't be a bear, as bears walk more quietly. I gingerly peer out from behind the rock.

It's a woman with golden-red hair that streams around her face and shoulders in the breeze, making her look like a wraith in the backlight.

She's tall and somewhat slight, and I now realize she knows I'm here, as she stops by the rock and looks my way. I can't quite make out her face, but I know the voice.

"Chinle, why are you hiding? What's taken you so long? I thought you would never get here."

It's Janie.

I know I'm dreaming, yet it seems so real. I step out from behind the rock, hesitant, yet happy to see her.

"Janie?" I ask tentatively.

She replies, "I've missed you, Chin."

I want to hug her, but something holds me back.

I reply, "Are you OK? I thought…"

"Yes, but I'm not really here, you know, not like I used to be, anyway."

I'm silent. I don't know what to say.

"Chinle, turn around and go home. You don't belong here. It's not a good place to wander. Go back to the desert, where you belong. You can wander there and be free. Go home."

"I have no home, Janie."

"Chin, home is where you choose to live your life story, where you belong. We all have a home. I came back to Alaska to die, dear cousin, but it really wasn't where I belonged, even though I was born and raised here. I belonged in Hawaii. You know where you belong, go home."

She turns, and the sun now shines directly on her. I recoil in horror.

She has no face.

The sun goes behind a cloud, and Janie turns and slowly walks away. As she disappears into the thick aspens, she becomes a blue glacier bear, loping away on all fours, her fur backlit as the sun comes back out, the same color as the beautiful pale-blue columbines we used to admire in the Colorado high country when she would come visit.

I'm now running back down the trail, frightened, but I'm soon forced to stop and catch my breath, and I think of Michio Hoshino, the Japanese photographer famous for his Alaskan bear photos.

Hoshino had a passion for photographing a glacier bear, but was never able to find one. Instead, he died filming polar bears in Russia, killed by one during the night in his tent, in spite of his friends trying to run it off. Ironically,

Hoshino loved bears and had been a world-wide advocate for their preservation.

As I pause on the trail, I look down to see huge bear tracks nearby. They look very fresh, and I'm quickly jogging again down the trail, even more wary, if possible, half looking over my shoulder.

Back to my truck, heart beating madly, I jump in and lock the doors, half expecting to see *Horribilis* emerge from the forest behind me.

Nothing.

Back in Palmer, the dogs greet me at the door as if they thought they would never see me again. I call my landlady to tell her I'm back. She tells me the neighbor was arrested for shooting at another neighbor for driving too fast. She seems relieved he's behind bars and will be staying there for awhile.

Haunted by my vision of Janie, I decide that I'll leave tomorrow, head back down that long highway, go back home, wherever that is.

RIDING THE WIND

The next day, I'm miles from Palmer, back in Tok, Alaska, when I get a call from Davie.

"Chin," he asks, "Everything OK?"

"Yeah, how about you?" I reply.

"Just checking in on you. I've tried to call several times, but you must've been out of range. Where you at?"

"I just arrived in Tok, Davie. I'm on my way back."

"I need to get back up there, it's been too long. Glad to hear you're on your way back. Say, um," he pauses, "I'm not really sure how to tell you this, but I got a call from Roddie, and, well, he um, well, Roddie had trouble getting it out, just like I am…Chin, are you driving? You might want to pull over for a minute. I don't want to lose you."

Davie sounds like he's about ready to cry.

"What's going on, Davie?" I ask gently, pulling into the parking lot by a gas station.

"Well, Roddie didn't want to tell anyone, but the coroner did an autopsy on Janie. It took a long time to get the results back, or maybe Roddie just took a long time to let us know what they were, I dunno…"

I answer, "Janie was mauled by a bear, so why have an autopsy? I don't understand."

"I didn't either, Chin, but I guess it's standard procedure. I mean, the EMTs, the doctors at the hospital, everyone said she died from a grizzly mauling, so why the coroner wanted an autopsy, I don't know. Probably Alaskan rules whenever someone dies in the wilds. But Chin…"

I struggle, trying to understand what's happening, knowing that soon Davie will tell me something I'll wish I didn't know. A bear mauling is simple, easy to understand—someone gets in the way of a bear and that's that. And even though it's a simple thing, a bear mauling, I'm still trying to wrap my mind around the fact that Janie's gone. I don't want to know any more, and I'm tempted to hang up, to tell Davie later that the connection dropped.

"Chin, you still there?"

Finally, I reply softly, "I'm still here. What happened, Davie?"

"Chin, Janie didn't die from a bear."

I suddenly flash back to the woman in Johnson's Crossing.

"Was Janie shot?"

Davie continues, his voice close to breaking. "Shot? No, Chin, she took her own life. Pills. Roddie said she had a fast-growing form of melanoma, and the doctors gave her only a short time to live. She didn't tell anyone, just went back to Alaska. She wanted to die where she was born. She took a bottle of pills and died there in the forest, all alone. A bear came by later and…well, it didn't kill her, she was already dead, or so the coroner said. It didn't even really maul her very badly. Probably just curious."

Davie pauses, as if still trying to control himself, then adds, "She was dead by the time the bear came by, and it didn't really do much to her body, that's why she was still back behind the rocks where she'd probably been sitting when she died. It's almost as if she'd hidden so no one would find her. A guy who was climbing off-trail was the one who found her, and he called the Alaska State Patrol on his cell phone."

I'm silent. How could Janie, who was always laughing, the one always there for me when I was down, how could she do this to herself, kill herself? It just wasn't possible.

"Davie, how does Roddie know all this?"

"It was in the goodbye letter, Chin. Before she died, she had letters for us all, but she never mailed them. It was almost like she thought she might change her mind. Roddie sent mine and yours. He mailed yours to me because he didn't know where you were. I just got them a few days ago, but didn't open yours. I've been on the phone with Roddie. He's having a rough time of it, as we all are, of course. Janie told me in my letter that she didn't want us all to worry and cry about her, she just wanted to be done with it and go, make it as easy as possible and not linger on. I admire her for it, but Roddie's having a tough go."

"Davie, would you do me a favor? Would you read Janie's letter to me?"

"Sure, Chin I can do that, but are you sure you're up for it?"

"No, but I need to know what she says, and being on the road will give me time to think about it."

"OK, hold on a minute and I'll go get it."

Davie's soon back. "Are you sure you want me to open this? There's something in it, like a necklace."

"Yes, I'm sure. What did she say in your letter?"

"Well, she basically just said she loved me and hoped I wouldn't hold this against her, but it was the right choice for her. She asked me to go spend some time with Roddie in Kaneohe and help him get through it all, as she knew it would really hit him hard, but she felt it would be better for him than watching her die in pain."

"Are you going over there?"

"I have a flight out tomorrow. I'll stay as long as he needs me. My daughter's going to take care of the dogs. I'm going to help Roddie spread her ashes off some mountain trail there she liked to hike on. Do you think you could come? Do you want us to wait for you?"

"I don't know, Davie. It would be awfully hard with the dogs and no place to leave them."

"I understand. Chin, you can come stay at my place while I'm gone. The key's under the front flower pot. I'll leave her letter on the kitchen table for you."

"How long will you be over there?"

"I'm planning on staying two weeks."

"I won't be back before you are, Davie, but thanks anyway. I'm going to come down the Cassier Highway, maybe go to the coast or something, then go on over to the desert for awhile."

"OK, but the offer stands. Anyway, here's her letter."

My dearest cousin,

You have always been the sister I never had, and I know the news of my death will be hard for you. We've always been so close, and I can only imagine what such news would do to me. I hope you can forgive me, but it's the only real choice I have. I have no hope, and the cancer is devastating my body. It will be a very painful ending, and I don't want Roddie or anyone to have to go through it with me.

I know that taking my life may make those who love me angry and possibly even bitter. I thought of telling everyone what I'm about to do so we could say our goodbyes, but sometimes such goodbyes are wrought with anger and indecision and questions such as why don't I fight it and win? There's no winning at this stage. Even the oncologist at Kaiser, one of the best, says there's no treatment that can kill it at this point. It has invaded everything, even starting to get into my brain.

I love you, and you will be on my mind up there in the beautiful forests of the Chugach, not far from where I was born and where I choose to die. It will be a peaceful death, and I will leave our beautiful planet as I came to it—alone. We are each alone, and this is a good thing, for we each have the power to design our own path and sometimes even how we will die. Being alone is not a curse, as some think, but an opportunity to discover who you truly are.

You will find a silver locket with this letter, one that you gave me when we were both 16. I've always treasured it, and in it you'll find a tiny sprig of blackbrush, one that you sent me from Utah. It was my reminder of you and the freedom you embrace, and I hope you can find a home, someplace where you're happy and content and where you can best live your story. That is my greatest wish for you.

All my love,

Janie

Everything now feels distant, and Davie's voice sounds as if it's floating on rays through the upper atmosphere, like scattered ions in the aurora. I feel alone, vulnerable, like a tiny speck of life in a vast universe spinning its way into oblivion.

"Chin, you still there?" Davie asks. "You OK?"

"I'm OK, Davie."

"She did the right thing for herself, Chin, even though it leaves the rest of us hanging. But we would've been left hanging regardless, no matter how we lost her."

"You're right, Davie. Thanks for reading that to me. It helps a lot. I hope you have a good trip to Oahu and can help Roddie. Give him my best. I'll be thinking of you."

"Chin, one last thing..." Davie pauses, then continues.

"Janie left us all some money. She left most of her stuff to Roddie, since he's her son. He said she'd just sold her travel business and made quite a bit from it. She left you and me each enough that I'm already talking to the guy who owns the little bungalow I rent here about buying it. And Chin, she left you enough for a nice house, too. Roddie said in her will she said she wants you to settle down or at least have a place for a permanent home base."

I'm silent. A house? My very own house? A place I can leave my stuff when I go wander and come home to? A home? Security?

I reply, "Davie, you're her brother. She should've left my share to you."

"No, it's OK, Chin. I didn't even expect anything. You know Janie and I weren't very close. We didn't have much in common. I'm lucky she left me what she did—she was very generous. Are you coming back now?"

"Pretty much, but it may take awhile," I reply, knowing that I now have one last thing I must do before I can return.

"Well, drive safe, and I hope to see you soon. Love you, bye."

Davie's gone, but I barely notice, for I have a new raison d'etre, something that has to be done to tip the scales of justice back where they belong, at least in my own mind.

I had intended to go back to the desert, but now I feel something tugging, opening up like the curtain on a stage, something new.

I now want to go to British Columbia's Great Bear Rainforest. It seems like a good place to see a bear, a good place to face my fears. I've built a giant malignment in my own mind, a false accusation, and it's time to tear it down.

Perhaps there in the rainforest I can regain my place in the natural order—I need to get over this irrational fear, the one that's been growing daily and taking over my life, my fear of *Horribilis*.

I let the dogs out for a few minutes, but a wind has come up, and they soon want back inside. Must be a storm brewing, maybe something coming in off the Aleutians. I'll have a nice tailwind, hopefully all the way into Canada.

I'll drive all night, even though the darkness only lasts for a few hours, watching carefully for wildlife, especially for woods bison sleeping on the warm highway.

I'll dodge moose and bison, riding the wind, listening to its stories as I drive along, stories of distant mountains and valleys I will never see, stories of people I will never know existed.

Like the wind, I'm driven by the Earth's turning, and I can somehow sense that another turning, another change lies ahead. I want to rewrite my story, knowing now that Janie's left me the money for a house somewhere, for a home.

Knowing she wasn't killed by a bear makes things different, and now my story can have a new ending, kind of like rewriting the words to a song.

URSUS ARCTOS
HORRIBILIS

Driving along, I think of bears and how I've became so obsessed with them.

My fear of bears began before Janie's death, maybe just a natural and adaptive fear of greater predators, but after she died I started remembering every story I'd ever heard about them, everything I'd ever read—and I soon realized I wanted to know how to avoid such a fate through an understanding of how people came to be killed.

Some of the stories came back to me in the middle of the night while sleeping there in my truck cab, even while out in the bearless desert, and I would roll up the window, knowing they were true stories.

For example, one particularly tragic story happened at Liard Hot Springs along the Alaska Highway in British Columbia. Because of this story, I decided not to stop there on my way to Alaska, even though it had happened some time ago.

I knew I wouldn't enjoy the hot springs, but would instead think about the poor woman from Texas who was mauled to death as her two children watched helplessly. An experienced bear hunter was also killed while trying to save her, as he had no weapon. Other tourists threw rocks but couldn't run the bear off. It was eventually shot by a tourist who kept a rifle in his RV.

The woman and her family were on their way to Anchorage to make new lives for themselves.

Then there was a story closer to home, as it happened in the same area where Janie was killed, in Chugach State Park near Anchorage. An older woman and her 45-year-old son were killed by a grizzly as they hiked a dense trail, and the woman's 14-year-old grandson escaped by climbing a tree. Bears rarely charge groups of people, but the hikers were hiking somewhat apart instead of together.

Wildlife officers found a partially buried moose carcass nearby and felt the bear was trying to protect its kill. Sterling Miller, an Alaska state research biologist, says that when a bear is defending something, it's not likely to be deterred by anything.

I think of the young forestry contract worker who was killed while working alone on Togwotee Pass in the Bridger-Teton National Forest in Wyoming. His death sparked controversy about letting forestry workers go into bear country alone, especially in an area considered to be part of the species' core habitat in the Yellowstone ecosystem. He wasn't carrying bear spray and apparently happened to stumble upon a cache of two deer carcasses.

And then I recall a story that some say is so outrageous it was made up, a story told by a half-native woman in Canada's Northwest Territory who had disappeared while morel hunting with a friend. The woman was an expert in the backwoods, so her friend only began to worry after she'd gone missing for a number of hours.

Nineteen hours later, the lost woman reappeared along with her dog, telling the Royal Canadian Mounted Police a story of being stalked by a starving wolf that drove her and her dog further and further into the woods.

Tortured by mosquitoes and with the hungry wolf getting bolder, she heard a cub calling for its mom and moved in its direction, hoping the sow would appear and scare off the wolf. The mother bear soon came to the cub's rescue, driving the wolf away, as the woman ran in the opposite direction, eventually making her way back to the highway.

To her detractors, those who thought she'd made up the story out of embarrassment at getting lost, the woman simply shrugged her shoulders and said she'd been searching for morels, not fame.

And so, the more bear stories I recalled, the more I came to realize that Alaska and Canada, especially B.C. and the Yukon, have plenty of such tales, and the more I came to realize that bear encounters can't be predicted. People have been mauled in their driveways, and bears have even broken into homes, as was the case with the woman at Johnson's Crossing.

Yet experts say that bear attacks are rare and that fatal attacks are even more uncommon. Stephen Herrero, a professor at the University of Calgary, has kept a database on bear attacks in North America that occurred since 1900. He maintains that the number of fatal attacks averages only one per year.

Eventually, I stopped reading about bears, as I found it too disturbing. But my trepidation of them grew, maybe because of their combination of intelligence and fearsomeness. Knowing that such attacks were rare made no difference. I also knew that bears were smart and could be predatory, a bad combination for us humans.

Gordon Burghardt, a professor at the University of Tennessee, says that bears are as intelligent as apes and learn things just as quickly. They have large brains and can see in color. His research shows that they can count and reason using numbers.

And Jennifer Vonk, a professor at Oakland University in Michigan, says that bears learn some skills even faster than apes and other primates. She's taught bears to use computer touch screens, selecting items with their noses and tongues, and has found that they quickly distinguish between different bear species as well as between photos of real animals and animal drawings. They are also clever at figuring out how to use drawers and sliding doors to get food from a box.

Stephen Stringham, an Alaskan bear researcher, says that bears have at least 20 different techniques for catching salmon, including sitting in a creek facing downstream, which creates an eddy that attracts fish.

We humans have always feared things that might be able to outsmart us, things that might have an advantage over us, whether it be in savvy, speed, sharper teeth, better night vision, cunning, or strength—things we often lack— yet in our hubris we declare ourselves the pinnacle of all.

We can relax, congratulating ourselves on our superiority, as long as we stay in groups, but we know that the bears are still out there, living their own lives in their own ways, in spite of our denial, occasionally reminding us of our folly.

I think of Charlie Russell, the bear conservationist who grew up on his parents' ranch in Alberta near Waterton Lakes National Park, and who lived among grizzly bears on Russia's Kamchatka Peninsula, adopting orphaned grizzly cubs, raising them and reintroducing them to the wild.

Russell's work there led him to the conclusion that grizzlies that trust humans, rather than fear them, are not dangerous. Back in Alberta, while his fellow ranchers were killing bears, Charlie would drag cattle that had died to a feeding place for the bears, who thereby left his stock alone—as well as him.

To Charlie, humans refuse to follow the laws of nature and have become too arrogant and privileged. He believes that living sustainably is the highest intelligence, and bears live sustainably, which humans generally don't. One can draw their own conclusions as to where Charlie stands on human versus bear intelligence, but he once said, speaking of humans, that he had trouble being courteous to a creature who thought it was superior to everything else.

* * *

These bear thoughts gradually fade, and all I know is the present, the hum of the engine as I pass through a world of forest and mountain.

The Chugach eventually make way for the Wrangells, their untouchable snowcapped peaks protected by hazy distance, which in turn make way for the St. Elias range. The magnitude of so many big peaks, so many unnamed mountains, makes me feel small and insignificant once again, and the endless wilderness brings on a hint of loneliness, of how it would feel to be the only human left in an endless immeasurable landscape.

I think of my own natural inclination to solitude and silence and wonder if I would be OK totally alone, if it would be sustainable. Complete solitude has driven some to madness.

But I do know that when you stand in the immensity of the natural world and realize how utterly insignificant you are, only then are you truly free.

I drive for a long weary time, and it's midnight before the lights of Whitehorse come into view. The sun has barely set, dipping below the horizon for a few hours. The solstice is near.

I think of Eddie the bull and another solstice in what seems long ago, a winter solstice in Green River, once my desert home.

Pulling off into a field behind the Berengia Museum, I pass by the world's largest weathervane—a DC-3 set on a specially engineered pedestal so it always turns into the wind, just as it once did when lined up on the runway for takeoff. I pull out my sleeping bag and snuggle down, dogs nearby.

As I drift off, I think I can hear a wolf in the far distance and wonder if it's actually a loon. I've heard coyotes making noise just for the fun of it, howling and yipping, and I wonder if wolves ever do the same. And what about bears? We know they play, both together and alone, but do they ever just sit and talk about things in bear speak?

I suspect that, unlike most humans, bears live their lives mostly in silence, listening to the world around them as well as to themselves, living the authentic life that seems to elude many of us. Not having a spoken language, bears tell no lies, but can they somehow tell stories?

I finally fall asleep, comforted by the sight through my pickup window of the stars in the Milky Way, Jupiter visible on the horizon, the northern sun soon to rise and obliterate it for another day.

FINDING YET ANOTHER PIECE OF MY HOME

The days again melt together into a hum of truck engine and wind whistling through half-open windows. Only the white and yellow stripes separate me from oncoming cars, which are few and far between. The Yukon is a place of vast distances—a vastness upon vastness.

Just before the town of Watson Lake is an intersection, an offshoot of the road less travelled onto a road even more less travelled, and I'm soon traversing the long thin line of the Cassier Highway, winding back into British Columbia through mountains bearing jade and gold and infinite thick forests. I lose track of the number of glacial-colored lakes and rivers, all like something from a landscape painting.

Finally outdistancing the Cassiers, I reach the small city of Prince George, where I resupply and spend the night tucked behind the shrubs of an overgrown parking lot at the edge of the city, shrubs that host endless hordes of hungry mosquitoes. These urban mosquitoes seem even more aggressive than the ones I've encountered in the wilds—maybe it's from feasting on human blood.

Continuing south, I'm now in Canada's Caribou Country, on the edge of the mighty volcanic Chilcotin Plateau. I eventually arrive in the town of Williams Lake after passing though the lumber-processing town of Quesnel and stopping at the local park there on the banks of the mighty Fraser River.

Canadian rivers seem massive and deep compared to the rivers of the American southwest, even when the latter are bank full in flood stage.

I gas up again, then turn west onto Highway 20 where a sign points to a mysterious place 379 km away bearing the melodic name of Bella Coola. This remote highway crosses the Chilcotin between the Fraser River and the Coast Mountains, where the highway then loses its pavement and drops off the edge of the earth at a place called simply "the Hill" by the locals, though it's officially known as Heckman Pass.

Many groups of First Nations peoples inhabit this part of British Columbia—the Chilcotin is home to the Tsilhqot'in and Dakelh peoples (which includes the Chilcotin group), while over 20 separate groups inhabit the Great Bear Rainforest, including the people of the Nuxalk Nation (pronounced "Noo-halk"), who live in Bella Coola, as well as the Heiltsuk of Bella Bella.

When Scottish explorer Alexander MacKenzie came this way in 1793, he found the natives to be friendly and peaceful.

The Chilcotin has only this one highway traversing it, with occasional gas stations in small native towns with few tourist services, towns with names like Tatla Lake, Kleena Kleene, Nimpo Lake, Anahim Lake, and Atnarko.

Chilcotin means "People of the Red Ochre River," which, along with the name, "The Rainbow Range," refers to the colorful volcanic activity that shaped the area. The Rainbow

Range is an extinct shield volcano with intense and varied colors from heavy mineralization.

Non-native ranchers also inhabit the plateau, which has herds of wild horses that are possible offshoots of the large herds acquired by the Okanagan and Nez Perce and other plateau peoples to the south.

As I leave Williams Lake, a sense of trepidation pushes away my sense of adventure, and I wonder if this new tack I've embarked upon will turn out to be a boondoggle, if my lack of planning will finally catch up to me. All I know is I'm going to drive almost 300 miles across a remote plateau in a remote Canadian province, then possibly drop into the sea.

I then shake my head at myself, thinking of MacKenzie, a real explorer, who crossed the Chilcotin with his six companions with no idea where they would end up. And then I go even further back, to the early natives, the early relatives of Kwaday Dan Ts'inchi, people who worked their way down the coast from the north, though some native legends say they arrived from the South Pacific on rafts.

My trepidation is borne by the dark clouds I see in the distance, or maybe it comes from an offhand comment someone made at the gas station in Williams Lake—apparently there have been a number of thefts recently from tourists on the Chilcotin, with the suspects being young First Nations men.

Given the poverty that accompanies losing one's subsistence lifeway, I'm not surprised to hear that some are resorting to theft.

But as I drive along, my fears fade, and the Chilcotin finally takes hold of my mind. I feel a sense of comfort in its semi-arid rolling hills, tall grasses, remote ranches, and herds of free-roaming horses. Something about it reminds me of where I was raised in northwest Colorado, my home as a child.

After many hours of driving, the tallest points of the Coast Mountains begin to poke up on the distant horizon, and I become more excited at the thought of seeing Bella Coola first-hand.

I arrive at the village of Anahim Lake, which has a feel to it that something interesting is about to happen. Perhaps it's the nearby colorful Rainbow Range that hints that one is nearing the western edge of the Chilcotin, or maybe it's the touristy flavor, with trucks pulling fishing boats, and signs for a lodge at the nearby lake.

Stopping for gas at a well-worn station, I go inside to pay, where an older woman, hair pulled taut against her head in a pony tail, introduces herself as Joan and asks where I'm from.

Her blonde-white hair and high cheekbones tell tales of ancestors who once roamed and pillaged by sea, and I suspect that she's a descendent of the many Norwegians who settled this area, descendants of Vikings, enticed to the area by offers of free land from the Canadian government.

She warns, "Be careful out there camping, this is grizzly country. I used to ranch with my husband, though he's now long gone. We spent many nights out there in our old canvas cabin tent."

I don't ask if her husband is long gone by choice or through death, though given her age, I suspect the latter.

Joan continues, "Sometimes the bears would come up to our tent and swat a little at the side, push the tent in, just to see what it was, then they would go about their business."

She rings me up and hands me my change, three Canadian dollars—a toonie and a loonie—then looks out the window.

"Now, if you have dogs, that might be another story, as bears don't like dogs, but I think you'll be OK. My daughter and son-in-law own a lodge over by the lake, and they take clients out on horse-packing trips all summer and never have any problems, except when they run into a bear that associates people with food. Keep your food away from where you sleep and tie it up where the bears can't get to it, and don't cook in the clothes you sleep in. But to just stop near the road and camp for the night, you should be OK. Are you going to Bella Coola or are you staying here at the lake?"

Upon learning that I'm going all the way to the end of the line, she cautions me about gearing down on the Hill and not riding my brakes.

She then adds, "You really should just go stay at my daughter's lodge for the night. She'll let you camp there on the grass with your dogs if you want. I just heard yesterday that another tourist got robbed, this time in Tweedsmuir. Nobody gets robbed in the park there, at least they didn't used to. Someone's been breaking into cars while people are out hiking."

"Do they know who did it?" I ask.

"Oh, yes, they know. It's the same bunch—a group of na'er do wells, the same ones who wish we'd all go away and give them everything we've worked so hard to estab-

lish here over the years. Problem is, nobody will do any-
thing about it. It's political and that's about all I can say.
Young punks. But be careful, especially out there alone.
Just go stay at the lodge, dear."

"Thank you for the offer, but I think I'll just keep going. I'm thinking I can get to Bella Coola by dark and camp
there. It's safe there, isn't it?"

"Oh yes, it'll be safe there. That's Nuxalk territory.
You're going to be driving the Hill after dark though, but
maybe that's the best way, as you can't see how far down it
is. But someone said there's some construction there, so be
cautious. If you see an old gray pickup, steer clear. There's
four of these hoodlums—two ride in front and two in back.
Don't be afraid to use your bear spray on them if need be—
if you don't have any, they sell it over at the store. Be safe,
dear."

I drive off, mulling over what she said about bears and
thieves, making me feel even more unsettled.

The highway turns to gravel at Anahim Lake, and I
haven't gone more than five miles when I have a flat. It's
my first flat in years, and I have to dig under all my gear in
the back to find my bottle jack.

I crawl under the truck to set the jack, but it seems to
be broken, as the handle won't turn. I groan, knowing full
well my serendipity has turned into carelessness—I should
check my gear more often.

I hear a vehicle pull up. I can see from my vantage point
that it's a gray truck, and I wonder if I shouldn't just stay
under my pickup, where I might be safer. I realize that, as
usual, my bear spray is nowhere nearby, but is buried in
my gear in the cab. I crawl out and stand up.

A middle-aged man, a First Nations native, stands in front of an old gray pickup, and a native woman and child wait in the cab, none of them looking much like they're out to rob anyone.

"You need some help?" the man asks. "I hope you have a spare."

I shrug my shoulders in frustration, pointing to the bent jack.

"I have a good jack," he replies, getting a scissor jack from the bed of his truck. He soon has my tire off, then releases the spare from its brackets and mounts it. He's quickly done, and I can tell he's changed many spares—and from the looks of the nearly bald tires on his truck, there will be more in his future.

"I don't know how to thank you," I say. "I would've been stranded out here with a broken jack."

"Someone else would've come along," he replies, holding out his hand and adding, "I'm Sesyaz. That's my wife Jennie and son Lake. We're from Bella Coola. Is that where you're going?"

"Yes, I was hoping to get there tonight. Can I pay you something? I don't want to insult you, but you're help has been invaluable."

Sesyaz laughs. "Yes, it would insult me. You can repay me by coming to visit us when you get to Bella Coola. We actually live in Four Mile. Just ask for Sesyaz Pootlass and anyone there can point you to our house. We would be honored to show you our home, yet another piece of your home. We Nuxalk people have a saying that all the Earth is our home, and one finds a piece of home wherever they go."

I pause, thinking of what he's just said, then go to the back of my truck and rummage through my gear.

"Here, I'd like for you to take this. I got it in Alaska." I hand him a pound of Tundra Mud, espresso grind.

"Thank you," he says. "We love good coffee. It's a very nice gift. We're on our way to Williams Lake to see the doctor. My son has an ear infection. We'll be coming back through here tomorrow. If you're prepared to camp, I would recommend staying up here, as the Hill is partially closed from rockfall. It'll be a little hard to drive in the dark, as it's one lane where they're working and somewhat exposed. You'd be better off waiting. Maybe we'll see you tomorrow on our way back, but if not, be sure to come visit us."

Sesyaz and his family are soon gone. I let the dogs out and shake my head at my luck, still trying to process how easily I got out of that one, especially with a broken jack.

Janie used to tell me that I always landed on my feet, and this time, it's true.

Pure luck, if there is such a thing.

OVER THE EDGE

The twilight has begun, and even though it lingers for a long time here in the North, I know I should find a place to camp.

Driving on down the highway, I know the Hill is near—I can feel the breathtaking depths where the Chilcotin drops into a rugged coastline of granite cliffs and airy waterfalls, where cold winds blast off lofty glaciers and brush across inlets filled with dugout cedar canoes. I can almost smell the wet mists of the many deep fjords below.

I find an old road and pull off into a clearing, then get out, shivering, even though it's not cold. I feel like I'm on the edge of the world, perhaps the edge of a new life, a new story.

And tonight, as part of the healing I'm hoping will now begin, for the first time since Janie's death, I will sleep in my tent, even though I know that a large percentage of people killed by grizzlies were in sleeping bags.

When bears become habituated to people and associate them with food, they usually will simply leave when nothing to eat is found, but sometimes such a bear, if hungry enough, will become predatory. They then see a human in a tent as easy prey, which they usually are, unless they have bear spray. A gun doesn't work as well, as usually the bear is upon you before you can use it.

The safest place one can pick to sleep is a place where bears don't go, where your likelihood of meeting one are slim to none. My pickup qualifies better than most places, certainly better than a lush meadow by a lake or a frequented bear trail, but I'm feeling more and more like I want to stretch out and sleep under the stars—if I leave my tent fly off, I can watch for meteors through the netting, as well as bears.

I can quickly slip out of my tent and into the truck if I camp next to it. I trust the dogs to alert me to anything strange—at least I'll be awake if a bear eats me.

I pitch my small tent, feed the dogs a ways from camp, then make a cup of tea, leaning back on my sleeping bag to watch the stars come out. But I'm fast asleep before it's even dark, which comes around 11 p.m., as I'm now much further south than Whitehorse.

It must be about three a.m. when I'm abruptly wakened from a deep sleep by something soft touching my head through the side of the tent, pushing the nylon up against me.

I hold my breath in fear, briefly wondering why I was foolish enough to think I would be safe in the middle of some of the wildest bear country in Canada. And for the briefest of moments, I see Janie's face and wonder what her last few minutes of life were like, even though I now know she wasn't killed by a bear.

Whatever it is backs off for a moment, then pushes again, this time a little harder, and I turn over and quickly unzip my bag, ready to make a quick exit, even though I know I could never outrun a bear, especially a grizzly, which can run up to 30 m.p.h.

Weezee and Cassie start growling, good guard dogs that they are, now that I'm already awake. Whatever is outside lets out a loud snort, and I fumble with my headlamp and the nylon tent zipper at the same time, cussing myself for leaving my bear spray in the truck.

Just then, I hear the sound of something heavy kicking up dirt clods, followed by the rapid clip-clop of hooves, quickly fading into the distance.

Horses! Probably some of the herds that roam freely across the plateau.

Just like the bears Joan told me about, they're curious. They must have come upon us in the night and wondered what my tent was.

I get my bear spray, then settle back into my bag, wide awake, and though it's only 4 a.m., I can see the first hint of dawn to the east, a deep blue etching the far horizon.

I'm still for a long time, acutely aware of any sounds, listening as a car passes on the nearby highway and fades into the distance.

The stars hang above me, telling tales of distant worlds, worlds I will never know, and soon a meteor streaks across the zenith, leaving a pale yellow phosphorescent line in its wake.

I awake a few hours later at dawn with a vague memory of a large white horse looking down on me through my tent's mesh top, and I wonder if it was a dream.

Brewing coffee on the truck's tailgate, I wonder if I should wait for Sesyaz and his family to return from Williams Lake. There was something about him, a presence that radiated competence and an ability to deal with anything, and the daunting road ahead makes me wish for companions to help see me through. I wonder if he's some kind of Nuxalk leader.

But there's no telling when he and his family will return, and I'm anxious to get going, so I finally load up the dogs and go on my way, thinking of the gray pickup Joan told me about and not wanting to press the good luck I've had so far.

A sign soon informs me that I've entered the southern portion of Tweedsmuir Provincial Park, and soon thereafter the pavement ends and another sign simply reads, "Heckman Pass," with no hint of the myths and fears associated with the name.

I get out at a viewpoint, looking down a wide glacial valley cutting through the Coast Mountains, dropping 5,000 feet below to where the Bella Coola River scours its deep course to the sea, finally finding its freedom.

I'm on the crest of what some call Cascadia, a long stretch from Alaska to California that follows the Cascadia coastal subduction zone. Bella Coola is a land of earthquake stories, with quakes that have been greater than the 7-point range on the Richter Scale.

And now, here at the top of Heckman Pass, rated by some as one of the more dangerous roads in the world, I stand at the door to the Great Bear Rainforest, the pass below me serving as a gravel gantlet for those with vertigo and who fear heights, dropping many thousands of feet—with no guard rails.

It's also called the Freedom Road, as it was built by local volunteers in 1953 who wanted a road to connect them to the mainland, giving them their freedom to come and go as they pleased, no longer having to rely on air or sea passage. Provincial authorities had decided that building the road would be too expensive and difficult and refused to help, though the government later paid those who built the road and agreed to maintain it.

The road took over a year to build, with two bulldozers starting from each end, hoping to meet somewhere in the middle. In places it's still only wide enough for one vehicle, and safety etiquette dictates that the one going downhill must back up to make way for the one coming up, as it's more dangerous to try to back downhill, as you don't have your gears to stop you, nor can you see as well.

The road has since been improved (it originally had switchbacks with 18 percent grades but now has 11 and 12 percent grades), but it's still famous in the annals of spectacular descents, giving those who manage to drive it a sheer sense of accomplishment and lifetime nightmares, though the locals think nothing of it.

Back in my truck, I gear down and remember what Joan said about not riding my brakes, though I've driven many such roads in Colorado, just not as long. I soon smell something burning and come to a car sitting in a pullout, the distinctive smell of burning rubber emanating from it as its driver waits for the brakes to cool.

As I wind down the thin ribbon of road, I can see the influence of the Pacific Ocean on the foliage as the semi-arid makes way for the subalpine then gradually becomes temperate rainforest with thick stands of Douglas fir, western red cedar, western hemlock, and stately Sitka spruce.

Concentrating on the road, I try not to think about the sheer drops, especially when I get to the stretch where a rockslide has narrowed the road to one lane. For some reason, I think of Davie and the rough road into the Dolores Triangle. Unlike Janie, who seemed cut out for the more civilized life, Davie likes challenges, and I suspect he would like this road. Maybe someday I can come back and drive it with him.

I'm suddenly on pavement again—I've reached the bottom of the Hill, and the only problem now will be going back up again, where one is in the outside lane, though that will be a challenge for another day. I've heard stories of people afraid to take the road back up and instead flying out of Bella Coola or taking the ferry.

Now farmlands line the road in the glacier-carved valley below snow-capped peaks and granite ramparts, and I know that in about 50 miles I'll reach the tidewater of the Bella Coola inlet.

On my way, I'll drive through towns with names like Stuie, Firvale, and Hagensborg (a Norwegian settlement), as well as native towns with soaring totem poles bearing the likenesses of ravens and other animals honored by the Nuxalk culture, including spirit bears.

And when I'm almost to Bella Coola, I'll come to the Nuxalk village of Four Mile, where I'll ask for Sesyaz Pootlass.

But first, I have some trees I want to visit.

INTO THE DEPTHS

Sometimes casual words can change the course of one's life. Such words can be our own or suggestions from others. For example, saying we're going to do something can create direction where there was none before, even if we hadn't really thought about it much until then.

There's something about changing thought into speech that gives it life, and what we say and what we don't say can have incredible power on the direction our life moves.

And so, we create storylines for our lives through sparks of intention that can grow into wildfires until we put them out by the doing of the thing, by following this new narrative we've constructed for ourselves. And such sparks can eventually burn and shape our history and the histories of other lives.

I don't recall where I first heard of the Great Bear Rainforest, nor do I remember it making much of an impression on me at the time, but upon hearing of Janie's suicide, I somehow told myself I was coming here, even though I had no idea why.

And so here I am, soon to enter the depths of an old-growth forest, the result of a random thought back near

Whitehorse, a decision to try a new path that rejected my fear of bears, a fear that Janie's death had magnified.

This is how we create the paths of our lives, most often through casual happenstance than not, though we like to think we have more control than that.

Somewhere along the way I had heard about K'iid K'iyass (Old Tree), the Golden Spruce, a mighty Sitka spruce tree growing on the banks of the Yakoun River on Haida Gwaii, the island of the Haida People, not all that far from Bella Coola as the raven flies. Haida Gwaii is part of the archipelago once called the Queen Charlotte Islands, known by some as the Misty Islands.

The Golden Spruce was an old tree born in the mists before the time of Columbus, over 1500 years ago, a tree highly regarded by the Haida and old enough that it had become part of their oral tradition. Like the Kermode, or spirit bear, its color was the result of a genetic mutation, although this tree bore no similarly colored offspring, unlike the Kermodes.

Because the tree had only 20 percent of a normal Sitka spruce's amount of chlorophyll, its needles were golden yellow instead of green, making many wonder how it could survive on such a meager diet. In addition, it was also perfectly cone shaped (most spruce grow asymmetrically), and had a trunk over six feet in diameter. It was a staggering 164 feet tall.

The Golden Spruce was cut down in 1997 by, ironically enough, an ex-logger named Grant Hadwin trying to make a statement about how destructive the logging industry in British Columbia was. Felling the tree was no mean feat, something only an expert logger could accomplish, given the tree's size.

Hadwin had begun to exhibit signs of mental illness, and his brother, who had schizophrenia, had committed suicide earlier. Somehow, Hadwin, an expert forester, must have thought it ironic that the logging companies left the chlorotic misfit Golden Spruce while cutting down all the healthy trees.

Arraigned by the authorities for criminal mischief and with a bounty on his head by the Haida and half of Canada, Hadwin rented a sea kayak and started from Prince Rupert to the site of his trial on Haida Gwaii. His route crossed Hecate Strait, one of the most dangerous passages in the world.

Hadwin's sea kayak was found months later on a small southern Alaska island. An expert survivor, some speculate that he didn't die but instead engineered the remote kayak crash so people would leave him alone.

And though I know I can now never see the Golden Spruce, I want to see its cousins, the huge 1,000-year-old western red cedars and Sitka spruce, some with a circumference much greater than that of the Golden Spruce— some up to 50 feet around.

I turn off the highway into Snootli Creek Regional Park and am soon on a trail winding through an ancient cedar grove, a place as foreign to me as my beloved Colorado Plateau desert would be to people like Sesyaz.

The Great Bear Rainforest receives over 65 inches of rain per year as the atmospheric flow of moist air off the ocean collides with the Coast Mountains. The deserts of the Colorado Plateau are lucky to receive six to ten inches a year.

In addition, the weather along the coastal rainforest is generally mild all year, making for a long growing season, though occasional strong winds can dip down from the Chilcotin. The plants that grow in the high deserts of Utah and Colorado must be adept at not only surviving with little moisture, but in surviving temperatures that swing from subzero colds to highs of well over 100 degrees.

As I follow the path through the wet forest, I wonder if the trees here ever know what fire is. The giant sequoias in California need fire, as the heat opens their seed cones and clears the forest, making room for the big trees, who stand unscathed by flames as other species around them perish. In addition, the cones of the lodgepole pine are sealed with a resin that can only be melted by fire, releasing the seeds.

I stop, wondering where the sunlight went. Looking up, I see a canopy of swooping branches—I'm standing under a giant cedar tree that appears to be at least 40 feet around, which would make it a seedling in the time of the Roman Empire.

I turn to see another, then yet another of the ancient trees, and a breeze picks up. They whisper to each other, perhaps warning of the interloper. Do these ancient ones know how many of their kin have been killed by humans like me?

A voice behind me says quietly, "Some say the trees scream when they're felled."

I turn, recognizing the voice—it's Sesyaz.

He adds, "I saw your truck and knew you were here. I don't mean to be depressing, but many come here and talk about how much timber there is and how many nice big cabins they could build. Some of us believe the trees have senses and can feel things much as we can."

"How's your son?" I ask.

"He's fine. The doctor gave him antibiotics. He's sleeping and seems much better today."

"That's good," I reply. "I was hoping I would run into you guys again."

"Yes, I'm on my way to my gallery."

"You're an artist?" I ask.

"Yes, I carve. I make totem poles. Small ones for tourists and large ones for the Nuxalk. We use them as territory and grave markers. The tourists use them to remember that this is another part of their home. I also carve ceremonial masks."

Sesyaz now leans back, looking up into the trees, silent.

Finally, I ask, "Have you ever heard them scream?"

"No," Sesyaz answers. "But I would never fell one."

"Don't you use them for the totem poles?"

"Yes, but I use only ones already dead. But I know a couple of loggers who say they've heard them scream. One told me that if you were to spend enough time among the forest giants, you would become aware of the groans and shrieks as they're felled. And I was in a pub in Williams Lake one day, back when it was a loggers' bar, and there was another First Nations guy there. He was drunk and started crying, saying he was quitting his job as a faller because he couldn't take the screaming of the trees any more."

I'm silent, taking in the filtered light, the thick ferny undergrowth, the mosses on the rocks. It feels like a cathedral, almost like one shouldn't talk.

I'm reminded of standing on the shores of the Yukon River near Whitehorse during break-up, and of how the ice shattered against itself, groaning and moaning as if alive and unwilling to let go of its security and float to new adventures. I then wonder if the Golden Spruce screamed when Hadwin felled it.

I ask in a very soft voice, "Did you ever see the Golden Spruce, Sesyaz? Over on Haida Gwaii?"

"The Old One. No, but my wife's best friend is from there, and she saw it many times. She's Haida, and the tree was sacred to them."

"Why did it grow so big when it was sickly?"

"She said it flourished because it was on the bank of the Yakoun River, which reflected sunlight into its understory of green needles. Those green needles provided the tree with nourishment. It was a very unique setting, allowing it to grow for centuries."

I nod my head, wondering if we humans, a bit chlorotic ourselves, are headed for a similar fate, one where we're cut down by our own hubris.

"Come by the house later," Sesyaz says, turning to go. "I'll be back in a couple of hours. I can loan you my kayak if you want to go see some of the really big trees across the bay. Your dogs will be OK for a few hours in our big fenced yard. The Spring Salmon Moon is almost upon us. Maybe you'll get lucky and see a spirit bear."

VALLEY OF DREAMS

I'm not a strong swimmer, not having grown up around water, and I've only been in a sea kayak a few times when visiting Janie in Hawaii, so it's with great trepidation that I slip into Sesyaz's kayak.

He's given me directions, of a sort, to what he claims are the biggest western red cedars and spruce in the Bella Coola area.

"It's pretty gentle waters here," he reassures me. "Just go to the trees, then come right back. But we do get some pretty bad afternoon winds that can make for high waves, though you'll be fine for a few hours. The cedars over there are huge. I would like to go with you, but I only have one kayak."

The water gently slaps against the sides of the boat, as Sesyaz continues.

"See that little point there? If you go past it, you're too far. Even though it's still a ways off, you don't want to go into the big channel. Takeout spots are sparse, so pay attention and don't hesitate to turn around anytime you feel uncomfortable. Where Burke and Labouchere Channels meet is Mesachie Nose, a Nuxalk word meaning "Dancing Waters." Winds strike the cliffs there and the waves rebound, causing rough waters. When there's a large ebb tide, there's trouble, that's why you must stay away. We'll have a meal ready when you get back—smoked duck with dried blueberries."

With that, Sesyaz turns and is gone, leaving me in a foreign world, a world that's home to him.

I push out away from the shore, getting a feel for the currents, gently turning the kayak this way and that to get used to how it handles. My fears are soon replaced by a combination of tension and exhilaration, and I'm reminded of how Davie described his first season as a wildland firefighter back in his younger days.

"It's a combination of fear, excitement, and wondering how in hellsbells you ended up there," he'd told me. He worked the fires for a number of seasons, helping him get through college.

I have no idea how I got here and never would have predicted it. I know that anything to do with water is second nature to the Nuxalk, and Sesyaz couldn't possibly know how foreign kayaking is to me.

I'm soon torn between a strong irrational urge to go back and an equally strong desire to see the big trees, even though I know I really have no business being out in such deep unstable water.

Before I know it, I'm quickly out in the main channel of the long, narrow, deep inlet, surrounded by vertical snow-capped mountains that drop straight into the sea. Very few takeout places, indeed! I see virtually none, as the thick forests end in cliffs that dip straight into the waters.

I feel a surge of water and suddenly find myself going the wrong way down the channel. Relieved, I think that the waters have decided it's best for me to return to Sesyaz. I suddenly want to be back on terra firma more than anything else in the whole world.

But just as quickly, the kayak turns, spins a few times, and is caught up in the outward current again and heads back away from shore. My meagre paddling skills, learned on a calm ocean in Hawaii, are slowly coming back to me, and I manage to turn the kayak towards the small point Sesyaz had pointed out as my destination, which can't be more than two miles away.

It now dawns on me that any place with names like Dancing Waters and Windy Bay might be the wrong place for a beginning kayaker. I think of Hadwin kayaking across Hecate Bay in a heavy storm and wonder if he felt like I do, for even though he was a better kayaker, he still was no expert.

I want to turn back, but instead continue on, some kind of compulsion driving me, maybe a similar madness to that of Hadwin.

Soon, I've triumphantly landed on a small stretch of sandy beach with a footpath going up into the trees, and I know I've made it to the ancient grove. I feel a great sense of relief, perhaps more from knowing I can now turn back with impunity than from knowing I can now visit the trees.

Careful to not get lost in the hanging mosses and bent branches and rocky wet rivulets running through everything, I sit under the largest tree I've ever seen, one with a girth that seems to project upward from within the earth, a geologic anomaly rather than a plant, giant furrows in its trunk looking like eroded fins in some strange formation.

And as I sit at the ancient giant's feet, I ponder the meaning of what it's like to be rooted, to never go anywhere else but the one spot you were born in. I think of all the people living in houses in the same town every day, and I think of Janie wanting to return to her birthplace to die.

I suddenly feel claustrophobic in the thick mossy forest and jump up and run to the kayak, nearly tripping on countless roots and ferns and tangled plants.

Soon in the boat, I push myself out to sea, headed in the direction of home.

Home.

Right now, Bella Coola is home, where the dogs and Sesyaz wait. Right now, home simply means safety and the comfort of being with my friends, Cassie and Weezee. And right now, I want nothing more than to be home. I don't want to be rooted, I want to be free to wander and roam, yet I paradoxically need the comfort of home.

The current is strong, but I'm gaining and can clearly see the point where I left Sesyaz. Unexpectedly, it begins to sprinkle, and I realize that the high clouds that had calmly rested for hours on the flanks of Nusatsum Mountain are now drifting down to the bay, bringing what look to be heavy rains with them.

Soon, mists swirl around me, visibility decreasing by the moment. And no matter how hard I paddle, it now seems as if I'm losing, for now the winds have come in and are pushing me backwards.

It occurs to me that, unlike Janie, I'm not going to be able to pick where I die. And it also occurs to me that I may never be found, just like Hadwin was never found—for a huge wave has nearly upended the kayak, catching me by surprise and taking my paddle, and I have no spare.

HORRIBILIS

Sometimes when I wake, I don't know where I am. I may think I'm where I was the previous day, which may or may not be true, or I may go back a week or even a month or year. It's a very disconcerting feeling.

And I now feel that way, though I haven't slept. Instead, I've been buffeted by ocean waves that broke far above my head, tossed and turned in blinding spray, and buffeted me until I'm surprised the kayak is still afloat.

But I have no idea where I am, just that I'm still in a kayak and the storm has passed, leaving trails of soft streamers breaking across incredibly high mountains, so high that even when I tilt my head back I still can't see their summits. I can see that evening is coming on from the pink alpenglow on their flanks.

As the mists rise to where I can see around me, I realize I am no longer out to sea, but am instead tangled in a web of roots along a shore that breaks into a small meadow of tall sedges.

I carefully climb from the little boat, hanging onto it for dear life until I've pulled it up out of the water. Maybe I can find something that will serve as a paddle and somehow get back home.

I begin looking for a suitable piece of wood, but everything's all wet and tangled and covered with moss and rocks and mud.

Mud bearing huge bear tracks.

Before I even have time to process the thought, I'm looking up the bank into the face of something very large and very pale.

A beautiful creamy-white Kermode bear, Ursus americanus kermodei, looks down on me with an expression of puzzlement, as if to say, "Why are you here?"

I stand, spellbound, frightened, speechless, and the thought of trees screaming when felled passes through my mind. Here, right in front of me, not more than ten feet away, stands a bear, and though not *Horribilis*, his cousin.

I think of all my fears, all the nights spent half-awake, worrying about bears, of all the images of what it must be like to be mauled and even eaten by one.

The bear stands, watching, as if waiting for me to make the next move.

And now, my fear is quickly pushed out by an overpowering sense of peace.

"Hello, bear," I say calmly. "Your frothy cream color reminds me of cappuccino, which I could sorely use right now, along with a kayak paddle. I'm sorry to disturb you."

The bear studies me for a moment, then turns and walks away, melting into the thick forest at the edge of the small clearing, its creamy-white coat blending with the white flowers of a thick stand of red elderberry bushes. Two black cubs emerge from the thick brush and run after it.

I'm dreaming, I think, yet the tracks are there in the mud, quickly filling with water. A mother bear with her two cubs, and she didn't threaten me.

And I know now I will never fear bears again, though I will always exercise great caution around them. This was no *Horribilis*, no grizzly, and who knows if things would have ended differently if it had been. But still, it was a mother with her cubs, a large bear, and she could have easily killed me.

But now, a voice startles me. I turn around to see a flotilla of six kayaks, and in the nearest is a man who has an air of authority, like a guide. He has a Canadian accent.

"Say, we thought we saw a spirit bear along here. Did you see it by any chance?"

"A spirit bear?" I ask.

"Yes, it's cream-colored, the Kermode bear, found only in the rainforest here. You've never heard of them? That's the main reason people come here, to see the spirit bears."

I think of Sesyaz and the Nuxalk people's regard for the spirit bear, and I have no desire to see these people come ashore trying to sight it, bothering the bear and her cubs even further. She might not be quite so patient with them.

"I saw a black bear," I reply, truthfully, as it actually was a black bear, just of a different color, and her cubs were black, the white gene remaining recessive.

The guide replies, "Oh, well, are you OK? You look kind of tossed around or something."

"I lost my paddle. Would you happen to have an extra?"

"You're out here all alone? And with no spare paddle? Well, OK, I won't preach, you can borrow my extra. I'm going to recommend that you come back with us."

"Thanks for the offer, and I think I'll take you up on it."

"Where did you get the kayak?"

"A guy in Bella Coola."

"Well, that little storm that came through earlier was something else, and I suspect it caught you, didn't it? We saw it coming and holed up along shore. We normally don't take this route for our tours, but we were on our way back and someone thought they saw a spirit bear over here. Otherwise, we would have never found you. You're very lucky, I hope you realize."

I reply, "Yes, I am very lucky. Now I can go home. Thank you for your help."

Everything seems a blur, but I'm eventually back to Bella Coola, where I meet a very happy Sesyaz, who I suspect had worried that he would not only lose his sea kayak but would gain two dogs.

I have a delicious meal with his family and give his son my coffee cup from Utah with Fremont petroglyphs on it. Sesyaz then gives me one of his small carved ceremonial masks, then offers to take me to see the famed Nuxalk petroglyphs. In return, I tell him I will someday buy him a new set of tires, which he finds amusing.

I camp in his yard, and the next day, after a hike to see the petroglyphs, I decide to catch the ferry instead of driving home, eager to get back to the desert. My luck holds, as the ferry comes only every few days, but I can leave that same day.

Down at the dock, I drive my truck into the hold, then leave the dogs in the cab with water and blankets. Though I'm not supposed to, that night I sneak my way down below, where I sleep with them.

I arrive in Port Hardy on Vancouver Island 17 hours after leaving Bella Coola, then work my way down to Victoria, crossing by ferry to the port of the City of Vancouver.

Working my way back east along the border, I eventually cross at Nelway into Washington, then drive through Pend D'Oreille country into Coeur d'Alene and on over to Missoula, then eventually on into Utah, where this story will end.

And with each highway mile, I begin to realize that like that small percentage of salmon who don't return to their place of birth, I will never be happy staying in one place, and unlike Janie and most salmon, I have no desire to die where I was born.

Every day and every night, I find a new home, and I'm content with that, as it's the life I live, my story. But I do know the landscape of my best home, and it's composed of desert rocks and ravens and scrub juniper and pinyon trees and sweet-smelling cliffrose. I may wander other landscapes, but I'll always return there, home.

And so, finally, one morning I wake, at the top of Soldier Summit, almost back.

It seems as if I've been sleeping for a long long time, but it's barely dawn, and I can still make out the handle of the Big Dipper, now almost touching the horizon. The Milky Way is now but a faint spray across the zenith.

The dogs jump out of the truck behind me, snuffling through the bushes as I make a cup of coffee. I sit on the bumper and watch as golden sunrays shoot across the sky like the Aurora Borealis.

I imagine I hear wolves howling in the far distance, and I have a vague memory, something that seems to touch the very tip of my consciousness, something that I can't quite make out, something perhaps like a large cream-colored bear dancing beneath Northern Lights.

I strain to remember, then give it up as being the traces of a lost dream. But somehow, I feel a comfort that's eluded me for a long time, the comfort of knowing my home isn't relegated to just one place, but is instead an entire landscape, and if I wish, an entire planet. Like the Nuxalk, I find a piece of my home wherever I go.

Now sun's rays strike a small patch of desert far in the distance. I stand and hold my arms wide, as if to embrace the scene before me, knowing the story will soon end.

And I know that the interest of a story isn't in its uniqueness, but is rather in the commonality of it, the portions we share with others. What's most important is seeing how to work your way through your own story and make it end well. We live in circles, coming and going, but in the end, we all return to where we belong.

Back in the truck, the dogs and I head on down the pass, back to our beloved desert.

Back home.

EPILOGUE

Perhaps we have overrated roots as a psychic need. Maybe the greater urge, the deeper and more ancient is the need, the will, the hunger to be somewhere else. —Steinbeck

While on my way to Davie's, I receive a call from Roddie, asking for my banking information so he can deposit the money Janie left me. It's only then that the whole idea seems real.

I eventually buy a cottage in Utah, then outfit it with a bed and other accoutrements of civilization, like a down comforter, a couch, and an espresso coffee pot.

I buy colorful rugs for the floors, then paint the rooms the hues of a desert sunset, the colors of a cobalt-blue raven's wings, the shades of redrock in moonlight.

I place my memories on the wide wooden windowsills—a small piece of jade from the Cassiers, a raven feather from the Green River Desert, a chunk of black tuff from Mt. Sneffels, a piece of blue-gray granite from the Yukon, Sesyaz's small ceremonial Nuxalk mask—and Moki's dog tag.

I make prints of some of my favorite photos, pictures I've taken throughout my wanderings—mostly of ravens, rocks, and sunsets—and hang them on the walls, along with a photo of Janie and Davie and me, taken at Halloween when we were just kids.

Davie and I wear headbands with feathers and carry toy bows and arrows, our faces painted like fierce warriors, but Janie's dressed like a Hawaiian hula dancer.

I send enough for new tires for his truck to Sesyaz Pootlass in Bella Coola, then donate the remainder of the money to a bear rehabilitation place in Colorado, where it will go to feed orphaned cubs.

Davie buys the place he's been renting in Grand Junction, where he retires from his job and becomes a wildlife painter.

My house is a cozy place and exactly what Janie would've wanted for me, though I'm seldom there.

But when I am at my base camp, which is most often during some big storm, I sit and read a book about someone's adventure somewhere, drinking tea by the little gas fireplace in the living room, where the walls are painted the rich deep greens of the Great Bear Rainforest.

A beautiful painting by Davie of a creamy-white Kermode bear looks down on me with an expression of puzzlement, as if to say, "Why are you here?"

I look up and reply, "I'm waiting for the skies to clear, my friend, then I'll be back out, following that unbroken line of freedom down some endless highway, looking for yet another piece of my home, for a new story to tell. And when I feel lonely out there, I'll think of how impossible it can all sometimes be, and I'll just come back home."

Then I close the book and take a nap, dreaming of a large spirit bear, its creamy fur glowing with burgundy highlights under the rare red lights of the Aurora Borealis, its big paws holding a map with long black claws pointing to my next adventure, while its two black cubs look on.

www.ingramcontent.com/pod-product-compliance
Lightning Source LLC
Chambersburg PA
CBHW062144280526
45788CB00001B/292